"Rob King and Eric Ferris invite you to have an easygoing conversation about the Holy Spirit. With clarity, deep insight and clever wit, they help us to take steps toward a faith that embraces the possibilities God has for us on this side of Pentecost."

Vincent Bacote, Ph.D., director, Center for Applied Christian
Ethics; associate professor of theology, Wheaton College

"An inspiring and helpful resource! For a topic that we often want to avoid rather than engage, Rob King and Eric Ferris demystify the Holy Spirit and provide a healthy framework for understanding how to truly live in the Spirit."

Jenni Catron, founder, The 4Sight Group

"Effortlessly moving between biblical wisdom and practical stories, *The Spirit Within* puts into words the longing we have for more. It's honest about what's confusing and clear on how to move forward. It is accessible for believers at every point in their faith walk and doesn't alienate people based on their theological background. It's a tall order to write a book about the Holy Spirit that's encouraging, informative, challenging and invitational. These authors have pulled it off, and if we put into practice what they te we'll be a stronger and more powerful Church."

Beth Guckenberger, co-executive dire

"King and Ferris accomplish an incredib
new book. Masterfully blending their ow
with almost seamless execution, they offe   .iat help
us delve deeper into our understanding of   .oly Spirit. Their
winsome prose, coupled with their rich theological dialogue, make
The Spirit Within a satisfying read from cover to cover."

Rev. Jason Brian Santos, Ph.D., mission coordinator
for Christian formation, Presbyterian Mission Agency,
Presbyterian Church (U.S.A)

"Rob and Eric invite followers of Jesus to wrap their arms around God's whole Jesus-gift. Written in an everyday, relatable style, *The Spirit Within* warmly and humorously guides readers to recognize, to engage and to depend on God's Spirit for abundant living and empowerment for Gospel mission."

Joel Willitts, Ph.D., professor of biblical and theological studies and practical theology, North Park University

THE
SPIRIT
WITHIN

THE SPIRIT WITHIN

GETTING TO KNOW THE PERSON
AND PURPOSE OF THE HOLY SPIRIT

Rob King
and Eric Ferris

Chosen

a division of Baker Publishing Group
Minneapolis, Minnesota

© 2019 by Rob King and Eric Ferris

Published by Chosen Books
11400 Hampshire Avenue South
Bloomington, Minnesota 55438
www.chosenbooks.com

Chosen Books is a division of
Baker Publishing Group, Grand Rapids, Michigan

Printed in the United States of America

ISBN 978-0-8007-9952-6

Library of Congress Cataloging-in-Publication Control Number: 2019018986

Unless otherwise indicated, Scripture quotations are from the Holy Bible, New International Version®. NIV®. Copyright © 1973, 1978, 1984, 2011 by Biblica, Inc.™ Used by permission of Zondervan. All rights reserved worldwide. www.zondervan.com. The "NIV" and "New International Version" are trademarks registered in the United States Patent and Trademark Office by Biblica, Inc.™

Scripture quotations labeled AMP are from the Amplified® Bible (AMP), copyright © 2015 by The Lockman Foundation. Used by permission. www.Lockman.org

Scripture quotations labeled CEB are from the COMMON ENGLISH BIBLE. © Copyright 2011 COMMON ENGLISH BIBLE. All rights reserved. Used by permission. (www.CommonEnglishBible.com).

Scripture quotations labeled CEV are from the Contemporary English Version © 1991, 1992, 1995 by American Bible Society. Used by permission.

Scripture quotations labeled CSB have been taken from the Christian Standard Bible®, copyright © 2017 by Holman Bible Publishers. Used by permission. Christian Standard Bible® and CSB® are federally registered trademarks of Holman Bible Publishers.

Scripture quotations labeled ESV are from The Holy Bible, English Standard Version® (ESV®), copyright © 2001 by Crossway, a publishing ministry of Good News Publishers. Used by permission. All rights reserved. ESV Text Edition: 2016

Scripture quotations labeled GNT are from the Good News Translation in Today's English Version-Second Edition. Copyright © 1992 by American Bible Society. Used by permission.

Scripture quotations labeled KJV are from the King James Version of the Bible.

Scripture quotations labeled MESSAGE are from THE MESSAGE, copyright © 1993, 1994, 1995, 1996, 2000, 2001, 2002 by Eugene H. Peterson. Used by permission of NavPress. All rights reserved. Represented by Tyndale House Publishers, Inc.

Scripture quotations labeled NASB are from the New American Standard Bible® (NASB), copyright © 1960, 1962, 1963, 1968, 1971, 1972, 1973, 1975, 1977, 1995 by The Lockman Foundation. Used by permission. www.Lockman.org

Scripture quotations labeled NLT are from the Holy Bible, New Living Translation, copyright © 1996, 2004, 2007, 2013, 2015 by Tyndale House Foundation. Used by permission of Tyndale House Publishers, Inc., Carol Stream, Illinois 60188. All rights reserved.

Scripture quotations labeled NLV are taken from the New Life Version, copyright © 1969 and 2003. Used by permission of Barbour Publishing, Inc., Uhrichsville, Ohio 44683. All rights reserved.

Scripture quotations labeled TLV are taken from the Tree of Life Version. © 2015 by the Messianic Jewish Family Bible Society. Used by permission of the Messianic Jewish Family Bible Society.

Cover design by Darren Welch Design

Authors represented by The Steve Laube Agency

19 20 21 22 23 24 25   7 6 5 4 3 2 1

In keeping with biblical principles of creation stewardship, Baker Publishing Group advocates the responsible use of our natural resources. As a member of the Green Press Initiative, our company uses recycled paper when possible. The text paper of this book is composed in part of post-consumer waste.

green press
INITIATIVE

To Stephanie, D'Ann, Jenna, Michael, Peyton, Courtney, Erin, Caleb and Katie.

CONTENTS

FOREWORD

I try to read at least one book a year on the Holy Spirit. This is almost embarrassing to write, but I need that gentle reminder regularly that the Holy Spirit of God actually dwells within me and that I have access to His comfort, counsel and power. Books and messages on the Holy Spirit tend to help us find our way when we have lost our compass. *The Spirit Within* is that book for me this year—and one of the best, well-balanced books I have ever read on this subject.

As a brand-new 21-year-old youth pastor, I worked for John Wimber at a church called Yorba Linda Friends. John later became the leader of the Vineyard movement, which will go down in modern-day Church history as one of the greatest movements of God in the twentieth century. His kids were in my youth group. I shared meals and life with him. And yet, he would say, it was not until he became totally open to the fullness of God through the Holy Spirit that he saw God work so strongly in his own life and then around the world. *The Spirit Within* reminds us that we have access to that same powerful Spirit within our lives.

Rob King and Eric Ferris have a most remarkable ministry at Vineyard Cincinnati Church. When you walk on the campus, you sense the presence of God in a beautiful and vibrant way. These men and this church demonstrate what the Vineyard movement calls "the radical middle." When it comes to living our lives by the power of the Holy Spirit, these are leaders and a church that live out these words: "Who says we have to go to one extreme or the other?" To neglect the Spirit of God in our lives is to neglect what Jesus called "the greater things." To be reckless with the Holy Spirit and turn the Spirit into a carnival sideshow is also not right. The right way is to lean into the power of the Holy Spirit and not be afraid of the Spirit's work in your life and your church.

The result of being connected to the Spirit of God within you is what the Bible calls "the fruit of the Spirit," which is love, joy, peace, patience, kindness, goodness, faithfulness, gentleness and self-control. If someone is mean-spirited or lacks any of these beautiful fruits of the Spirit, then I think it is right for us to wonder if that person is truly in touch with the Holy Spirit working in his or her life. Rob and Eric call the fruit of the Spirit "the signature of a life filled with the Holy Spirit." I am not a theologian. My emphasis in ministry is the family. I have had the privilege of watching marriages be healed and children who were violating the family values come back to the faith because someone in the family called upon the power of the Holy Spirit.

Does God do miracles today? You better believe it. This may sound like an oversimplification, but miracles of every kind are happening all around the world, and they most often happen when God's people are grounded in the person and purpose of the Holy Spirit. Rob King and Eric Ferris are not only inspiring communicators, they also live out what they write. If you are like me and, at times, need a solid reminder of the Holy Spirit working in and through you, then this book is for you.

Jim Burns, Ph.D.,
president, HomeWord; author, *Doing Life with Your Adult Children:
Keep Your Mouth Shut and the Welcome Mat Out*

AUTHORS' NOTE

Throughout the pages of this book, the personal pronoun *I* is used in relating personal facts and anecdotes without specifying which of the authors is speaking. This is done simply to make reading easier.

ACKNOWLEDGMENTS

To Vineyard Cincinnati Church and the church staff. We love you and what the Lord is doing in you and through you!

ONE

THE QUEST FOR MORE

HOW CAN IT BOTHER YOU if it is not even there?

Maybe you have experienced it. Many people have reported the phenomenon. It was even given a name more than a decade ago.

One day, Heather, a mother of three from Pittsburgh, was talking on her cell phone to her mother—a regular occurrence. Suddenly, she felt her phone vibrate in her hip pocket, where she always kept it when not using it. She reached for her phone, but it was not in her pocket. She stood, but she had not been sitting on it. She spun and looked all around for several minutes as she continued her conversation with her mother.

"Ugh," she said finally. "I can't find my phone."

Her mother laughed.

"What?" Heather was sure she felt the phone buzz in her pocket, but now it was nowhere to be seen. "Why are you laughing?"

"Honey, how are you talking to me?"

Heather pulled the phone away from her ear and looked at it, shaking her head. She returned it to her ear.

"Wow, I'm an idiot," she said, and mother and daughter shared a laugh together.

It is called "phantom vibration syndrome," and there are many theories as to what causes it, though so far no one has settled it conclusively.

Many otherwise happy and mature followers of Jesus Christ report a similarly mysterious experience. It has nothing to do with cell phones or technology, however. Rather, it is a fleeting, lingering sensation that something is missing. Something important. Something more.

Lives of Quiet Dismay

In his classic work *Walden*, Henry David Thoreau said famously, "The mass of men lead lives of quiet desperation."[1] And hold the jokes right there; he was not just talking about married men. In fact, he was not even referring only to men. He intended to include the entire human race in that appraisal. He meant people. Everywhere.

But, you may be thinking, *followers of Jesus should not be included in such a statement*. Right? Some of us are seldom quiet, to begin with, but more importantly, those who have experienced new life in Christ ought to be the least desperate and most fulfilled people on earth. After all,

> The God and Father of our Lord Jesus Christ . . . has blessed us in the heavenly realms with every spiritual blessing in Christ. For he chose us in him before the creation of the world to be holy and blameless in his sight. In love he predestined us for adoption to sonship through Jesus Christ, in accordance with his pleasure and will—to the praise of his glorious grace, which he has freely given us in the One he loves. In him we have redemption through his blood, the forgiveness of sins, in accordance with the riches of God's grace that he lavished on us. With all wisdom and understanding, he made known to us the mystery of his will according to his good pleasure, which he purposed in Christ, to be put into effect when the times reach their fulfillment—to bring unity to all things in heaven and on earth under Christ.
>
> Ephesians 1:3–10

That seems like a lot to be happy about, right? I mean, come on:

The Father . . . has qualified you to share in the inheritance of his holy people in the kingdom of light. For he has rescued us from the dominion of darkness and brought us into the kingdom of the Son he loves, in whom we have redemption, the forgiveness of sins.

Colossians 1:12–14

What more could we ask for? Why should we ever feel defeated or dismayed or dissatisfied?

And yet, if we are honest, many of us do feel this way—at least at some level. We are forgiven, redeemed and blessed. We love God, we follow Jesus, we pray and read our Bibles and so on, but we still suffer from the spiritual equivalent of phantom vibration syndrome—an occasional sensation that something should be there . . . but it is not.

Maybe Jesus' first followers suffered from the same malady. On one occasion, a man brought his son to Jesus for healing. Jesus was not there, but the man located a few of Jesus' disciples. He told them that his son was possessed by a demon that had robbed the boy of speech and would throw him to the ground writhing, foaming at the mouth and grinding his teeth. So the disciples—who had been following Jesus for some time and had even witnessed, preached and traveled the countryside performing miracles in Jesus' name—tried to call the demon out of the boy. And failed.

Soon after, Jesus came onto the scene, and the father explained his son's predicament and the disciples' failed efforts. Jesus rolled his eyes. Okay, so the Bible does not say that. But it does indicate some exasperation on the part of Jesus, who then said, "Bring the boy to me" (Mark 9:19). The account goes on:

So they brought him. When the spirit saw Jesus, it immediately threw the boy into a convulsion. He fell to the ground and rolled around, foaming at the mouth.

Jesus asked the boy's father, "How long has he been like this?"

"From childhood," he answered. "It has often thrown him into fire or water to kill him. But if you can do anything, take pity on us and help us."

"'If you can'?" said Jesus. "Everything is possible for one who believes."

Immediately the boy's father exclaimed, "I do believe; help me overcome my unbelief!"

When Jesus saw that a crowd was running to the scene, he rebuked the impure spirit. "You deaf and mute spirit," he said, "I command you, come out of him and never enter him again."

The spirit shrieked, convulsed him violently and came out. The boy looked so much like a corpse that many said, "He's dead." But Jesus took him by the hand and lifted him to his feet, and he stood up.

Mark 9:20–27

In public, the disciples probably applauded. "Hooray! Hallelujah! Praise Jesus! Another one bites the dust!" But in private—as it often is with us—their reaction was different. More honest. "After Jesus had gone indoors, his disciples asked him privately, 'Why couldn't we drive it out?'" (Mark 9:28). They were thinking: *What did we do wrong? Why couldn't we do that? What are we missing?*

Reality Bites

Maybe you can identify with those first followers of Jesus. They felt a disconnect between their expectations and their reality. Sound familiar?

So it is with our sense of *something missing*. We know that Jesus promised many wonderful things to His followers and, to be fair, we have expected and experienced some of those wonderful things. But, honestly, our expectations have sometimes been dashed.

Jesus promised, for example, "Anyone who believes in me will do the same works I have done, and even greater works" (John 14:12 NLT). But, like those disciples confronted with the demon-possessed boy, we are usually left wondering, *What am I doing wrong?*

We sense that we should be feeling more comfortable and confident in our relationship with God, rather than riddled with doubt and unsure about who we are and where—or even if—we belong in the Kingdom of God.

Some of us feel at times as though we have lost our compass. It seems as if we used to see everything more clearly than we do these days, from the moral lines in the world around us to the lines between right and wrong in our own hearts and lives.

We thought by now—those of us who have followed Jesus for more than a few weeks—that we would be better in so many ways. Our prayers should be more frequent . . . and more often answered. Our Bible reading should be enriching and rewarding . . . and more regular. Should we not be better at resisting sin? Holier, even?

And those "greater things" Jesus mentioned. Would you not think they include miracles? Healing? Not just physical, but in our relationships, in our families? Should we not feel more capable, peaceful, joyful, spiritual?

Are we just complainers? Malcontents? Or is there really *something missing*? And if so, what is it?

FOR REFLECTION

- In what ways has your expectation of the Christian life differed from your experience of living the Christian life?

TWO

"I KNOW A GUY"

WHAT RICHES have you left undiscovered, unused?

John Cole lives not far north of Cincinnati. He once got a call from a friend who said he saw John's name on an unclaimed-funds website. So John went online and looked into it. Sure enough, his name was there, from a stock that he had bought for twenty dollars years before—one share of the Boston Celtics basketball team. The company had apparently gone private, but John had moved and the company could find no forwarding address. John had forgotten all about it, but his dividends had been accumulating year by year without his knowledge. So he downloaded the paperwork, mailed it to the address listed on the website and received a check several weeks later for $212.00, along with the now-worthless stock certificate.

Rick Nowlin was attending the University of Pittsburgh in the 1990s when he received a call from someone working for the state of Pennsylvania. The caller asked, "Did you attend the University of Pittsburgh?"

"I still do," Rick answered, and subsequently received a financial scholarship that he had never claimed. The scholarship was more than $1,000.

If you do not claim it, it does not matter if there is an account somewhere with your name on it. Similarly, many of us who are followers of Jesus do our best to live our lives, day by day and year after year, without drawing from the resources that already belong to us. We feel inadequate, insecure and deprived, looking in all sorts of places for relief when Jesus has already supplied the "something" that we feel is missing. Except it is not some*thing*. It is *Someone*.

A Good Guy to Have Around

On the last night before His execution, Jesus met for one last supper in the Upper Room with His closest friends and followers. He washed their feet. He broke bread with them. He predicted His betrayal and even indicated to Judas that He knew who His betrayer was. The meal was winding down, and Jesus knew that He would soon be arrested, tried, humiliated and crucified. But before all that, He had one last thing He wanted to teach. What was the last message Jesus wanted to say to His disciples before going to the cross?

We find it in the Bible, in John's gospel:

> "Do not let your hearts be troubled. You believe in God; believe also in me. My Father's house has many rooms; if that were not so, would I have told you that I am going there to prepare a place for you? And if I go and prepare a place for you, I will come back and take you to be with me that you also may be where I am."
>
> John 14:1–3

You see, the disciples had gotten used to being where Jesus was. They had been with Him almost constantly for three years, walking and talking together, eating together, sleeping nearby. They accompanied Him to weddings, funerals and banquets. They had seen Him turn water to wine, heal the sick, even raise the dead. He even helped them with their tax returns.

On one occasion, Jesus challenged Peter on the need to pay taxes.

"Hey, Peter, who pays taxes? The king's children? Or others?"

When Peter answered, "Others," Jesus gave him a strange assignment.

"Still, let's not offend anyone. So I want you to go fishing."

Peter must have thought: *I like where this is going.*

"And in the fish's mouth," Jesus added, "you'll find a coin and it will cover our taxes."

Jesus is a good guy to have around, right? Think about it. Taxes come due, Jesus takes care of it with a little fish fry. Who else would go for that at tax time? *Dear Jesus, hear our prayer.*

They learned to rely on Him.

On another occasion, Jesus had been teaching the crowds. People swarmed to hear Him and maybe see Him do something spectacular. On this particular day, thousands of people had gathered, and they had lost track of time until they started to get hungry. But one boy had brought a sack lunch, and one of Jesus' followers brought the boy to Jesus. The boy had to be hungry, too, I imagine. I used to be a boy, so I know. But one way or another, he offered it to Jesus. Jesus gave thanks for the food, broke the bread and handed the food to His followers, who distributed it to the crowds. And that sardines-and-cracker lunch fed thousands of people. The disciples even collected leftovers after that. It is good to know Jesus. People started following just for the free breakfast.

No wonder they started to rely on Him. They began to know that everything He said was right on target. They could count on Him to say the right thing and do the right thing. Every single time, every situation they encountered. He never had a challenge He could not meet, never an obstacle He could not surmount by the Spirit of God.

What is that, you say? Your brother died? No problem. Jesus is four days late? No, He is not. He is right on time.

Jesus came into town and told the funeral directors to roll away the stone from the guy's tomb.

They tried to warn Jesus, "Man, it stinks in there."

No matter. Jesus called Lazarus out of the tomb, and he stumbled out, still in the tightly wound grave clothes—but alive. They had to take the grave clothes off! Jesus raised him from the dead!

It is good to know this guy. Jesus is a good guy to have around. And the disciples understandably got kind of used to that. Who would not?

Years ago, when I lived in Houston, I had a friend named Don. He is still my friend. And Don is still his name. When I moved to Cincinnati to serve and teach at Vineyard Cincinnati Church, he and his wife came all the way from Houston and sat in the front row through all four weekend services just to smile at me and make me feel good. They are wonderful people and amazing friends.

Don is a contractor, so he knows everybody. He and I have long had a running joke between us because, you know, I talk for a living; I cannot really fix anything. Whatever goes wrong, I make sure it is totally broken so that we can pay somebody else to fix it. That is kind of my gift. And whenever something broke or malfunctioned, I would talk to Don and he would say, "Don't worry. I know a guy." Every time he said it, I just knew that "I know a guy" meant "We'll get it done."

Someone in Residence

Where was I going with this? My point is that Jesus' disciples had all gotten to the place where they could say, "I know a guy." Can you imagine what it was like to walk with Jesus every single day? Eventually, you would not answer any questions. You would just say, "Talk to the Man." So that was the context for Jesus' words in the Upper Room. It had been so good to know Him, to have Him there, to rely on Him, to know that whatever came their way, they "know a guy." So when Jesus said, "I'm going away"—can you imagine? They had to have been looking around the room, thinking: *Oh, this isn't good. What are we going to do without Him?*

But then Jesus explained what was going to happen when He left:

> "I will ask the Father, and he will give you another Helper, who will stay with you forever. He is the Spirit, who reveals the truth about God. The world cannot receive him, because it cannot see him or know him. But you know him, because he remains with you and is in you."
>
> John 14:16–17 GNT

Think about it. Jesus was saying, "I'm going away but I'm sending you someone who will not only be *with* you as I am, but also be *in* you, guiding you and helping you." The Greek word is *parakletos*, which means "someone who comes alongside." Jesus said that this *parakletos* would be with them, and He would even reside in them.

What if I told you that Jesus was coming to your house tomorrow morning, just to walk with you all day long, right there, robe, sandals, beard, everything, alongside you? It would be "Take-your-Savior-to-work day." Would it change anything? You might adjust the way you drive: *Jesus is in the car now. I better not say that. I better not do that.* If He were there for every conversation you had, you would be careful, right? You would be checking with Him. It would change the interaction you have with people. You would look to Him for wisdom. You would go on your lunch break and probably riddle Him with questions.

I have this situation I've been dealing with, Jesus, and I don't know what to do. Will You show me what to do?

Well, Jesus is saying, "I sent you another Helper, the Holy Spirit, who is not only with you but is *in* you."

If you have surrendered your life to Jesus and received new life by trusting in Him, you do not have to search for this Companion, this Helper. You do not have to invite Him or conjure Him up. He is already on the inside.

That is why Jesus could say, "It's good that I'm going away because I'm limited to time and space. But the Holy Spirit will be with you and will be in you."

It is like sharing a house or apartment with a couple of people. Once they take up residence, you stop inviting them in. You do not have to invite them because they are already living on the inside. Of course, you can share a home with someone and not have a good relationship. This may be particularly true when teenagers are in the house. Maybe not, but stay with me for a moment. If I am not careful, I can go days without any meaningful interaction with my teenage children. Nothing is wrong, necessarily. We love one another. We live under the same roof. We notice when the last potato chip or pizza roll disappears. But life gets busy. We have different schedules. We take each other for granted. When that happens, we need to exercise a little intentional attention and make the effort to talk to each other.

Such basics of good relationships apply to the presence of the Helper in our lives. He is there. He wants to help. But life gets busy. We need to exercise a little intentional attention, acknowledge Him and cooperate with Him.

One time, Jesus' followers were in a boat on the sea. The winds were raging and the waves were tossing the boat. But Jesus was not there. He had gone to the mountains to pray. They were on their own. Jesus eventually came to them, walking on the water, but those moments when Jesus was away from them must have been challenging.

But whereas Jesus was with them in one place at a time, the Holy Spirit would be with them—each of them—everywhere they went. And if you are a follower of Jesus, you have that Helper living on the inside of you.

What if Jesus had left it entirely up to us? What if He had waved at His followers as He ascended into heaven, saying, "Well, good luck. You all take it from here"? We would be in deep trouble.

What if you had only yourself to rely on? Have you ever tried to reach God on your own? Serve Him in your own strength? You know, just, "Bless God, I'm going to buckle down, grit my teeth and do it my own self."

No, you are not. You are not going to do it on your own. You cannot do it. No amount of effort can banish fears and instill faith. No amount of trying can give the assurance of salvation, the power of God's presence in your life, the ability to pray effectively, the hunger and thirst for righteousness, and the strength to resist temptation and live victoriously day by day. No "just-do-it-ism" will ever produce godly fruit in your life, make you more like the person God created you to be or give you the power and presence of mind to be used by God to lead others closer to God. That is not at all how God planned things.

As a matter of fact, after Jesus rose from the dead and His followers were all excited, He told them, "Don't go anywhere. Don't do anything. Sit tight. Wait until I send you help."

Why would we think it should be any different for us? As He did to His first followers, Jesus could say to us, "This Christian life is not to be expected or attempted without the Helper. That's why I have given you the Helper, and with Him will come the power you need to do all that the Father has put in your heart. But it won't be you doing it; He will be doing it in you and for you and through you. And then, as I have said, you will have life . . . and you will have it more abundantly."

FOR REFLECTION

- The Christian life is not to be expected or attempted without the Helper. In what ways have you tried to live the Christian life on your own?

- Why does it matter that the Holy Spirit is a "He" and not an "it"?

THREE

DEFUSING
THE FEAR FACTOR

FEARS ABOUND in modern life. There are many to choose from:

Ablutophobia, the fear of bathing
Acarophobia, the fear of tiny bugs
Acerophobia, the fear of sourness
Achluophobia, the fear of darkness
Acousticophobia, the fear of noise
Acrophobia, the fear of heights
Aerophobia, the fear of flying

And that is just the first seven on a list of phobias, which could be a problem if you suffer from heptaphobia, which is the fear of the number seven. Or if you have phobophobia—the fear of fear itself!

In fact, an up-to-date list of clinical phobias—fears recognized and indexed by mental health experts—names more than five hundred separate fears people have. These are real fears people deal with, fears that assail them, limit them, even cripple them. Snakes top the list, at 25 percent, followed by a fear of being buried alive, at 22 percent. I do not know about you, but to me, some of these are just common sense. (Can you imagine the fear of being buried alive *with* snakes?) I think there is something wrong if you are *not* afraid of some of those kinds of things.

But some fears are more common than others, and some control our lives more than others. One fear that fits both of those categories—common and controlling—is the fear of the Holy Spirit and His gifts.

Fear, Confusion, Apprehension? Oh, My!

Why would anyone be afraid of the Holy Spirit? You would think Christians, especially, would be immune to such fear. Right? Not exactly. And even when it does not rise to the level of fear, there often seems to be a lot of confusion and apprehension regarding the Holy Spirit.

I was raised in a Roman Catholic family. We worshiped at a Catholic church. I attended a school called Holy Cross. You know you are at a Catholic school when it is called Holy Cross. The only thing more Catholic than a name like Holy Cross is Sacred Heart. Maybe.

I am grateful for my Catholic heritage, even though I attended Holy Cross back in the day when they did not apply therapy as much as they did spanking. They just spanked you if you were bad and that was your therapy. I am not saying it was good, and I am not saying it was that way everywhere. I am just saying that is how it was for me.

When I was a Catholic schoolboy, we never heard anything about the Holy Spirit, at least not in my parish. God, of course. Jesus, yes. Mary, you bet! But the Holy Spirit? Not a breath. (See what I did there?) He did not even enter the conversation.

Then, one fateful Wednesday night, my parents visited a Pentecostal church service. Have you ever been to a Pentecostal church? Some people call them "Holy Roller" churches. Wild things can happen in these churches, at least from the perspective of a Catholic. People shouting. People dancing. People running, even rolling in the aisles. Maybe it was because a Catholic schoolboy tripped them. I am not sure.

I was eleven years old when my family joined the Pentecostal church, a place where the Holy Spirit was mentioned way more than Mary.

I remember hearing a sermon in that church about this thing called "the Holy Ghost." The preacher explained that the Holy Ghost could come and fill you up. Then he asked, "Do you want more of God?"

I did, even at eleven years old. So I went forward to the altar, little Robby King, and suddenly, I was surrounded by a group of praying people. Heavy hands were laid upon me. Hot hands. I remember how hot those hands were. People were speaking loudly and shouting.

Some of them were saying, "Just let go. Let go."

Another guy was saying, "Just hold on, hold on."

I did not know what to do. I was brought up Catholic, you know? I had no idea what I was doing, what was supposed to happen or what was going on.

It felt like a reverse exorcism in which they were not trying to get something *out* of me but rather trying to put something *in* me that evidently did not want to go there. They apparently knew I was an unworthy vessel, so their vigor and enthusiasm were probably justified. They needed all the help they could muster to get this Holy Spirit into me.

Then I figured out that the way they would know I got the Holy Spirit was that I would speak in another language, just as they did during their services. Man, oh, man, the pressure was on. So, I did it. I spoke in tongues. I do not know whether it was out of coercion, compulsion or something else, but whatever it was, it seemed to make everyone happy. But it only confused me.

Years later, when I returned to the Lord after a period of rebellion and wandering, one of the first things I did was to go to the Bible, praying, "Father, what do You say about Your Holy Spirit? Teach me what You want me to know."

Do I Have to Look Weird?

When I was in graduate school, studying social science, I heard the story of the blind men and the elephant. None of the men had ever encountered an elephant before, so they decided to enlarge their knowledge by examining the beast.

The first man found the animal's trunk and said, "Oh, an elephant is shaped like a thick snake."

The second man gripped the elephant's ear and said, "No, an elephant is like a giant fan."

The third man grabbed one of the elephant's legs, pronounced the first two men wrong and said, "An elephant resembles the trunk of a tree."

The fourth blind man placed his hands on the elephant's flank, saying, "An elephant is like a wall."

The fifth man clutched its tail and said they were all wrong. "An elephant is like a rope."

The last man found a tusk and declared, "An elephant is like a spear."

Of course, each man was correct. And all of them were wrong.

The illustration is far from perfect, but people often do something similar when they encounter the Holy Spirit or talk about Him. We bring unique backgrounds to the discussion. We approach Him at different points. We experience Him from varying perspectives.

And the result is often confusion, even fear.

The problem is that people tend to go to one of two extremes concerning the Holy Spirit. As soon as I say, "Holy Spirit," people bring all of their baggage to that name. Some of us think: *Well, God the Father, He's okay. And Jesus, He's really great. But the Holy Spirit is the crazy uncle of the Trinity. Yeah, I don't really know what to think about Him, so I don't want to talk a whole lot about Him. And some of the people I know who talk a lot about the Holy Spirit are the weirdest people on the planet.*

Sound familiar?

At one extreme, the Christian experience is perceived as one in which believers have angelic visitations every morning when they wake up. They go to Walmart and prophesy over the produce, maybe bless the dairy section and cry "Glory to God!" over the bread. They might get a word from God in the deli department and utter "Bless His name" to the butcher slicing the ham. On their way out, they lay hands on a store clerk who gets slain in the Spirit. It is a Pentecostal Power parking lot.

Can you see how some of us may be excused for asking, *Does the Holy Spirit have to make me weird?*

At the other end of the spectrum are my friends who grew up in churches that taught that once the book of Acts ended and all the apostles died, the Holy Spirit went into hiding. They were taught that the gifts of the Spirit mentioned in the Bible died with the apostles, and that today, speaking in tongues is actually inspired by Satan himself. Further, the Holy Spirit is not on the move, and if you think you feel the Spirit move, it is probably indigestion.

You may be new to the Christian faith, the Bible and the Holy Spirit. Or you may have been raised in a church where the Holy Spirit was largely ignored or neglected. You may come from a church background where they cry, "Hallelujah! Praise Jesus. Glory to God!" Whatever your background, I want to ask you to put it aside. Whatever baggage you may be carrying, whatever fears you have, I invite you to lay down those things and go to the Bible with me, praying, "Father, what do You say about Your Holy Spirit? Teach me what You want me to know."

Let's look to the Word of God and see what He has to say, because none of us has complete understanding. The Bible says:

> Now our knowledge is partial and incomplete, and even the gift of prophecy reveals only part of the whole picture! But when the time of perfection comes, these partial things will become useless. . . . Now we see things imperfectly, like puzzling reflections in a mirror, but then we will see everything with perfect clarity. All that I know now is partial and incomplete, but then I will know everything completely, just as God now knows me completely.
>
> 1 Corinthians 13:9–10, 12 NLT

There will be a day when we will know everything completely. Today is not that day. But we can do our best to discern, with the help of the Holy Spirit Himself, what God's Word teaches about the Holy Spirit. We may not have a complete picture, but we can pray, and as the Bible says, "When he, the Spirit of truth, comes, he will guide you into all the truth" (John 16:13).

The Signature of the Holy Spirit

I find it interesting that when Paul—the great first-century church planter and writer of two-thirds of the New Testament—composed the letter we know as 1 Corinthians, he wrote chapters 12 and 14 (as we know them) about the role and gifts of the Holy Spirit. But in between, he wrote chapter 13. Have you heard of it? Many people call it "the love chapter." It is often read at weddings. It begins:

> If I speak in the tongues of men or of angels, but do not have love, I am only a resounding gong or a clanging cymbal. If I have the gift of prophecy and can fathom all mysteries and all knowledge, and if I have a faith that can move mountains, but do not have love, I am nothing. If I give all I possess to the poor and give over my body to hardship that I may boast, but do not have love, I gain nothing.

Beautiful, right? It keeps going:

> Love is patient, love is kind. It does not envy, it does not boast, it
> is not proud. It does not dishonor others, it is not self-seeking, it
> is not easily angered, it keeps no record of wrongs. Love does not
> delight in evil but rejoices with the truth. It always protects, always
> trusts, always hopes, always perseveres. Love never fails.
>
> 1 Corinthians 13:1–8

What is all this talk of love doing between chapters that are filled
with teaching about the Holy Spirit? It is because love is, first and
foremost, the signature of a life that is filled with the Holy Spirit
(see Galatians 5:22).

If I told you that I had the spirit of Einstein, but I could not
balance my checkbook, would you believe me? Probably not.

Or if I said I had the spirit of Michael Jackson, even if I had
the glove, hat, cane, everything, but could not dance or remember
the words to "Billie Jean," you would say, "You've got some spirit,
all right, but it's not the spirit of Michael."

Am I right?

Because to have that spirit of someone is to be able to do what
he or she can do.

We can talk about being filled with the Spirit. We can talk
about having the gifts of the Spirit. We can talk about the power
of the Spirit. But if we are not living a life of love, we do not have
the Spirit or we are not yielded to the Spirit, because the fruit of
the Holy Spirit is love. The power of the Holy Spirit is the power
to love God, to love one another, to love all. And when we love—
guess what? The Bible says, "There is no fear in love. But perfect
love drives out fear" (1 John 4:18).

The Father loves you. Jesus loves you. The Holy Spirit loves
you. And He will pour love into you and through you. You do not
need to be afraid of what will happen when you live a life that is
filled with the Holy Spirit as you become more like the person God

created you to be. The Holy Spirit's intention is not to make you more weird; He wants to make you more loving.

Several years ago, I was called to pastor at Vineyard Cincinnati Church. I did not have a background in the Vineyard movement, so I had to do my homework. I quickly became a big fan of what the Vineyard calls "the radical middle." It is a thoughtful position that asks, "Who says I have to go to one extreme or the other? Who says I have to carve out my own personal theological position and defend it until I'm blue in the face?"

I know that others think entrenched positions at one extreme or the other are super important, but personally, I am happy to stake out a position in "the radical middle."

I have pastored at several different churches that have different styles and theological leanings. I was raised Roman Catholic, studied at an Assemblies of God Bible college, pastored in an inter-denominational church with charismatic leanings, pastored in a non-denominational church with Reformed theology leanings, pursued graduate studies at the mainstream evangelical Wheaton Graduate School and now am a pastor at a Vineyard church.

You know what that makes me? Confused.

No, not really. I am just a normal person whose life has been changed by a loving God. I want to be the person God created me to be, and I need the Holy Spirit for that to happen. If I could do it on my own, it would already be done. I want to understand the Bible so I can know God better.

Pinned against Extremes

I love amusement rides. Have you ever been on a gravitron? It looks like a giant flying saucer. You go inside and stand against the outer wall with a bunch of other people. The door closes and the gravitron begins to spin faster and faster. The faster it spins, the stronger the centrifugal force pushing you against the wall. The force finally pins you there and you just kind of stick. The fun of it is that people battle the force, trying to strike funny poses, but physics eventually wins. It is an exhausting ride. It is not too long before you are ready for it to be over.

As you are getting tired and looking and laughing at all the other riders, however, you notice that right in the center of the gravitron is the ride attendant just standing and watching with no problem. Standing right in the middle, the attendant is not subjected to the force, no matter how fast that thing spins.

Of course, the church is not an amusement park ride. My point is this: It is possible to stand in the middle. In fact, it is the only place to stand and not be affected by the forces trying to push people as far to the outside as possible.

I have learned from worshiping and working in many different church settings that most Christians share the same basic beliefs regardless of what church they attend. They want to understand the Bible, feel loved and live a life that honors God. From time to time, however, I come across folks who have succumbed to unhealthy extremes. They are pinned to the wall, and they want you to join them.

At one extreme are those who are so preoccupied with the Holy Spirit and the things of the Spirit that they do not have much time or respect for the Bible. At the other extreme are those who have great respect for the Bible and yet neglect the Holy Spirit. Either extreme is an exhausting and unhealthy place to live.

I invite you to join me in the "radical middle." Go ahead. Consider this a formal invitation. There is no need to be afraid of the Holy Spirit or of falling into the extremes surrounding Him. The Christian life is biblically informed and Spirit-filled.

I do not want to be boring. I do not want to be weird. I *do* want to know the Holy Spirit. I want to be guided by Him. I want to live a life that is filled with the Spirit, overflowing with love, one that makes me more and more like Jesus every day. I want to be patient and kind, not envious, boastful or proud. I do not want my life to dishonor others. I do not want to be self-seeking, easily angered, holding grudges. I want to rejoice with the truth. I want to live a protecting, trusting, hopeful, persevering life. I want a love that never fails.

How about you?

Father, help me, by the power of Your Holy Spirit, to learn what Your Word says. I don't want to go beyond it. I don't want to fall short of it. I want to be Spirit-filled, Spirit-controlled and Spirit-led. I want Your perfect love for me to drive out all fear and guide me into all of the truth. In Jesus' name. Amen.

FOR REFLECTION

- Where do you find yourself between the two extremes in the continuum below?

Preoccupation with the Holy Spirit	⊢————————————⊣	Fear of or ignoring "things of the Spirit"

- Why do you think that is?

FOUR

THE PROMISE
AND THE PACKAGE

THEIR LEADER KNEW the end was close, the moment when darkness would descend, hope would flee and He would die. He knew they would scatter in fear and doubt. So, during their final meal before His passion, Jesus told His closest friends and followers:

> "I will ask the Father, and he will give you another Helper, who will stay with you forever. He is the Spirit, who reveals the truth about God. The world cannot receive him, because it cannot see him or know him. But you know him, because he remains with you and is in you."
>
> John 14:16–17 GNT

It was a wonderful promise. He was about to leave, but He told His disciples, "Don't be afraid. I'm going to go away—but it's a good thing that I'm going away, because the plan from the very beginning has been that I will go away and then I will send you another Helper, who will not only be *with* you but will be *in* you."

Jesus' words apparently went over their heads at the time, but it was not totally new information. It had been promised much earlier. God had said through the prophet Ezekiel, "I will give them an undivided heart and put a new spirit in them; I will remove from them their heart of stone and give them a heart of flesh" (Ezekiel 11:19). It had been the plan all along.

When God led His people out of slavery in Egypt, He instructed Moses, "Have them make a sanctuary for me, and I will dwell among them" (Exodus 25:8). There, in the holy of holies at the center of the Tabernacle—an elaborate but portable tent—the presence of God dwelled among His people.

Centuries later, after King David had made Jerusalem the capital and center of worship for God's people, King Solomon built the Temple there, praying, "I have indeed built a magnificent temple for you, a place for you to dwell forever" (1 Kings 8:13).

But even that glorious Temple did not fulfill God's ultimate plan. All along, the plan was for Jesus to take on human flesh and "tabernacle" among us (see John 1:14 TLV), then die for our sins, rise from the dead, ascend into heaven and send the Helper—the Holy Spirit—to live in His followers. This is why Paul wrote to his fellow Christians, "Do you not know that your bodies are temples of the Holy Spirit, who is in you, whom you have received from God?" (1 Corinthians 6:19).

This is also why Jesus could tell His followers, "It's *good* that I'm going away, because like the Tabernacle and the Temple, I'm limited to time and space. But the Holy Spirit will be with you and will live in every single one of you."

Jesus, in His human flesh, could be in only one place at a time, but the Holy Spirit can be with us everywhere we go. While Jesus, in His flesh, was subject to the limitations of time and space, the Holy Spirit has no such limitations. That was the plan from the very beginning.

Today, I have good news for you: If you have received Jesus Christ, you have the Holy Spirit living on the inside of you. But if you have not taken that step of believing in Jesus and accepting His offer of forgiveness, cleansing and deliverance from sin, you can do that right now, wherever you are. You can speak a simple prayer, sincerely saying:

"Jesus, I am a sinner like everyone else in the world. I am sorry for the wrong things I have done, and I want to turn away from following my own worst impulses and follow You instead. Please forgive me. Cleanse me from guilt and shame. Remove my stony heart and give me a new heart. Put a new spirit in me—Your Holy Spirit—who will be with me and live in me and help me to follow You the rest of my life. Amen."

If you have surrendered your life to Jesus Christ, He has given you the Holy Spirit, who is the Helper He promised. That means you have help living the Christian life. It is not on your shoulders alone. Jesus did not leave it entirely on you.

As we said earlier, Jesus did not wave at His followers as He ascended into heaven and say, "Good luck. Hope it works out for you." We are not left merely to read the Bible and do our best. We do not have to muddle through any way we can. Maybe sometimes it feels that way to you. If it does, you need this book (which is good, since you are already reading it). You need to learn how to have a great relationship with the Person of the Holy Spirit.

After all, He is living within you.

The Promise

What Jesus told His earliest followers is also true of us. He said, "I'm not leaving you as orphans. I'm not leaving you alone. I'm going to be with you, and here's how I'm going to do it. The Holy

Spirit is going to be with you forever, and He is going to live inside you. Always. Forever."

His promise, "I'm sending you another Helper," assumes you need help. We all do. None of us can live the Christian life without help. We cannot do it on our own. There is no amount of effort that is going to get it done. No declaration of "Bless God! I'm going through no matter what!" There is no pulling ourselves up by our bootstraps. We cannot grit our teeth hard enough to do it.

That is not how it is done. That is not God's intention. He wants us to lean on Him, to be filled with His Spirit and to let Him guide us and provide for us, being constantly and totally dependent upon Him.

We noted earlier how, after Jesus rose from the dead and appeared to many of His followers, He told them, "Don't go anywhere. Don't do anything until I send you help."

They did not fully understand what that meant, of course, until the "mighty rushing wind" came on the Day of Pentecost and they received the Holy Spirit. But they did what He said. They waited. They did not head out on their own. They did not buckle down, get fired up and launch out to try to change the world against all odds. If they had, they would have failed.

Jesus says the same to us: "Don't try this Christian life without the Helper. But when the Helper comes . . . man! You're going to have a new heart and new power and you're going to be My witnesses. But this is the way that you're going to do it. You're going to do it the way that I've planned it out from the very beginning and orchestrated it. You'll have the Helper, the Holy Spirit, living on the inside of you."

The Package

The relationship of the Holy Spirit to the Father and the Son was vividly displayed at the baptism of Jesus. When Jesus was baptized by John the Baptist, He went under the water like everyone else who was baptized that day. When He came out of the water, however, the Holy Spirit descended like a dove and alighted on Him. And then a voice from heaven said, "This is my Son, whom I love; with him I am well pleased" (Matthew 3:17).

What an amazing scene displaying the threefold nature of God! The Son is God, but He is not the Spirit or the Father. The Father is God, but He is not the Son or the Spirit. The Spirit is God—are you following me?—but He is not the Son or the Father. Each is distinct but they are a unity.

We often learn about unity at an early age. When you were growing up, did you ever pit your parents against each other? Did you ever go to one of your parents and ask, "Hey, can I do such and such?"

Which parent was it? Because there is usually one pushover parent and one strict parent. Of course, you did not go to the strict parent first, right? You went to the pushover parent in the hope that he or she would say, "Oh, yeah, sure."

And *then* you went to the strict parent and said, "Pushover parent said this is great."

And even if pushover parent was wise enough to say, "I don't know; go ask strict parent," you still went to the strict parent and said, "He said (or she said) it was fine, great, awesome. He's even willing to pay for it all and said for you to give me the money."

Great plan, eh?

Or maybe it was different for you. Maybe you did not have a pushover parent and a strict parent. So you might have played a different game. You might have come into the house and tested each parent's state of mind, gauging whether or not you could ask what you wanted to ask right now. What kinds of moods were they in? *Oh, Dad seems a little grumpy, but Mom's humming. She seems happy, so I'm asking Mom.* But if they were both in a bad mood, you bided your time. *Nope, I'm not bringing that up today.*

If it was urgent, you had to make the best of it. Maybe you complimented your mom's appearance or brought your dad his favorite snack as he reclined in his chair because it always seemed to work for the happy families on TV.

(I am writing from experience. When my kids come to me saying, "Mom said . . . ," I am ready: "Oh, no, you don't. We pulled that one way back in the '80s. I know this trick. I didn't invent it, but I perfected it.")

My point is, maybe you could pit your parents against each other, but you cannot do that with God. The Father, Son and Holy Spirit always know what is up with the others, and they are always a unit in perfect harmony. You cannot go to the Holy Spirit saying, "Don't tell Jesus this. All right, Jesus can know but don't tell the Father. I'd rather He didn't know. You know how He gets."

They are never in competition with one another. They are never jealous of one another. As a matter of fact, they always prefer one another. There is a corporate humility among the Trinity, if you can believe that. The Persons who created and rule the universe have a corporate humility, always striving to serve one another and glorify each other. Humility is not just a trait that God wants us to have; it is a characteristic He possesses. He knows who He is. He is confident in who He is. And there is no competition within the Trinity, just perfect unity of absolute harmony. It is a beautiful picture of what the Church could be and should be.

That is why, when Philip told Jesus in the Upper Room, "Lord, show us the Father and that will be enough for us" (John 14:8), Jesus seemed a little frustrated. That was another occasion when, I think, Jesus rolled His eyes. I do not have any scriptural support for that opinion, but I think it is a safe inference in this case because of how Jesus answered Philip:

> "Don't you know me, Philip, even after I have been among you such a long time? Anyone who has seen me has seen the Father. How can you say, 'Show us the Father'? Don't you believe that I am in

the Father, and that the Father is in me? The words I say to you I
do not speak on my own authority. Rather, it is the Father, living in
me, who is doing his work. Believe me when I say that I am in the
Father and the Father is in me; or at least believe on the evidence
of the works themselves. Very truly I tell you, whoever believes
in me will do the works I have been doing, and they will do even
greater things than these, because I am going to the Father. And
I will do whatever you ask in my name, so that the Father may be
glorified in the Son."

John 14:9–13

Jesus was one with the Father, and the Father was in Him. Jesus
was conceived by the power of the Holy Spirit, led into the Judean
wilderness by the Spirit, descended on by the Spirit and blessed by
the Father at His baptism. Everything that Jesus did in His earthly
life, every word He spoke, He did so not on His own authority
or on a whim, but by the power of the Spirit to glorify the Father.

How did He know what to say? How did He know where to
go? How did He know that the water would hold Him up when
He went walking across it? All of that was the work of the Holy
Spirit. It is not because Jesus had some superhuman body, about
which some people mistakenly think, *Well, He's Jesus; He can
do anything.* No. Scripture teaches that Jesus—though He never
stopped being God—was fully man.

Who, being in very nature God, did not consider equality with
God something to be used to his own advantage; rather, he made
himself nothing by taking the very nature of a servant, being made
in human likeness. And being found in appearance as a man, he
humbled himself by becoming obedient to death—even death on
a cross! Therefore God exalted him to the highest place and gave
him the name that is above every name.

Philippians 2:6–9

What is this passage saying? He slept. He woke. He ate. He was flesh and blood just like us. Yet He was filled with the Spirit. And it was by the Spirit that He said, "I've been with you so long and you don't know the Father? You want to see the Father? If you've seen Me, you've seen the Father." It was a package deal.

You want to know what the Father is like? Look at Jesus. You want to know the Holy Spirit? Look at Jesus. You want to know how Jesus did all of the wonderful things He did—how He resisted temptation, spoke powerfully, healed lepers, walked on water and raised the dead? He did none of it by Himself, though He was (and is) the Son of God. He did it all by the authority of the Father and the power of the Holy Spirit. That is what Jesus previewed and promised to His followers—a promise that was fulfilled at Pentecost.

The Pentecostal Moment

Imagine what it must have been like for those first followers of Jesus to wait in Jerusalem for His promise to be fulfilled, the promise of a Helper who would be with them and even live in them. Sure, Jesus had risen from the grave. He had appeared to them and others. And He had ascended heavenward after promising, "You will receive power when the Holy Spirit comes on you; and you will be my witnesses in Jerusalem, and in all Judea and Samaria, and to the ends of the earth" (Acts 1:8).

So they waited. They gathered. They prayed. The women prayed with the men (which was a new experience for males and females alike). They conducted a little business, prayerfully selecting Matthias to take Judas Iscariot's place. But days turned into weeks and still they waited. They must have been sorely tempted to start a softball team or hold a bake sale just to pass the time.

But finally, it happened:

When the day of Pentecost came, they were all together in one place. Suddenly a sound like the blowing of a violent wind came from heaven and filled the whole house where they were sitting. They saw what seemed to be tongues of fire that separated and came to rest on each of them. All of them were filled with the Holy Spirit.

Acts 2:1–4

The Helper had come. He took up residence in each of them. He was not only *on* them or *with* them (as the Hebrew Scriptures described); He was *within* them. (We will discuss this further in the coming chapters.) That day marked a crucial turning point in their lives and in the history of the Church.

In his book *The Holy Spirit: Activating God's Power in Your Life*, Billy Graham tells a story (which may be apocryphal) of an Arctic explorer who, in that vast, icy and desolate land, wrote a short message, attached it to a carrier pigeon and released it to make the two-thousand-mile journey back home to Norway. The bird took wing, circled a few times and flew off on a wing and a prayer. Days later, the pigeon descended and dropped into the lap of the explorer's wife, who read the message and knew that her husband was alive.

Graham wrote,

Likewise the coming of the Holy Spirit, the Heavenly Dove, proved to the disciples that Christ had entered the heavenly sanctuary. He was seated at the right hand of God the Father, for His atoning work was finished. The advent of the Holy Spirit fulfilled Christ's promise; and it also testified that God's righteousness had been vindicated. The age of the Holy Spirit, which could not commence until Jesus was glorified, had now begun.[1]

Similarly, when you placed your trust in Jesus and experienced new life through faith in Him, the age of the Holy Spirit commenced for you. The Helper came to you. He took up residence in you. He was not only on you or with you as He was for the ancient judges and prophets. He was *within* you. Upon your soul's surrender to Jesus Christ, He started working immediately. He clocked in and is not going to clock out.

He is always at work, and He is at work in your life right now.

FOR REFLECTION

- What do you think when you consider that the Holy Spirit residing within you has been God's plan from the beginning?

- How does it make you feel that the three Persons of the Trinity (Father, Son, Holy Spirit) are in perfect unity, and that they work together in your life in complete agreement—sort of a "package deal"?

FIVE

LIVING CONFIDENTLY

FRITZ RUECKHEIM was a German immigrant and popcorn seller in Chicago who debuted a new recipe of popcorn, peanuts and molasses at Chicago's first World's Fair in 1893. After three more years of closely guarded experimentation, he produced and named the first lot of Cracker Jack. By 1912, a toy or prize was included in every box of Cracker Jack—from rings and figurines to booklets and stickers. Until 2016, when QR codes—barcodes on the boxes allowing games to be downloaded to the Cracker Jack app—replaced tangible prizes, everyone who opened a box of Cracker Jack also received something extra.

Though it may seem a frivolous comparison, the same is true of all who experience new life through faith in Jesus Christ. Everyone who opens his or her life to Jesus Christ receives something—or, actually, Someone—extra: the Holy Spirit. And with the presence of the Spirit in our lives comes numerous other gifts, which the coming chapters will unfold.

Our friend Raul Latoni[1] is the senior director for spiritual growth at our church, Vineyard Cincinnati. In a recent talk to our church, Raul said this:

I was raised in a great family from Puerto Rico. My father was a senator. My mother was an assistant to the Secretary of State in Puerto Rico. But having wealth, affluence and an education did not preserve me or protect me from the power of addiction.

At the age of fourteen, I started using drugs, and I continued to do that for many years. I came to the United States at age eighteen to go to college at the University of Massachusetts. I not only continued to use drugs there but started dealing drugs so that I could sustain my drug habit. One thing led to another, and it was a snowball effect.

Eventually I was transporting drugs between New York and Massachusetts, driving four hours with my car loaded with cocaine so that I could sell to dealers. I wasn't the biggest or the "baddest"; I was just lost in my sin.

On October 1, 1987, I walked into a small storefront church in Brooklyn, New York, in an area called East New York. If you know much about Brooklyn, you know that's a rough neighborhood. I had no particular reason to be there except that somebody had invited me.

But on that day, I walked in there and was gripped by the message of the Gospel. I heard about this God who was not distant but near, who had sent His Son to die for my sins. I heard that He would be able to forgive me regardless of where I was in my life because He had a new direction in mind for me. And on that day, I said, "God, if You are able to change my life, I will give You my life today."

And He did just that. As the Bible says, "God, being rich in mercy, because of the great love with which he loved us" (Ephesians 2:4 ESV), He made me alive in Christ. And from that day on, He has been walking with me. I would say that before that, I existed, but the moment I met Jesus Christ, that was life, and that was life abundant (see John 10:10). I'm so glad that our God is not only a saver but He's also a keeper. The Word of God says that "if the Son sets you free, you will be free indeed" (John 8:36).

When Raul experienced the freedom and blessing of new life in Christ, he—like everyone who does so—received the Holy Spirit. And one of the things the Holy Spirit does when He comes into our lives is to impress upon us that we have become children of God. He does this to make sure we know that we are adopted into God's family—that we belong to Him and He belongs to us.

The Bible says:

Those who are led by the Spirit of God are the children of God. The Spirit you received does not make you slaves, so that you live in fear again; rather, the Spirit you received brought about your adoption to sonship. And by him we cry, "Abba, Father." The Spirit himself testifies with our spirit that we are God's children. Now if we are children, then we are heirs—heirs of God and co-heirs with Christ, if indeed we share in his sufferings in order that we may also share in his glory.

Romans 8:14–17

Romans 8 is unique because in the space of seventeen verses, the Holy Spirit is mentioned sixteen times. No other passage of Scripture is quite like it in making clear to us some of the ways in which the Holy Spirit works in our lives.

Raul provides a fitting analogy:

As I said before, I am of Puerto Rican descent, and if you know Puerto Rican people, you know that we come in all shapes and sizes and colors. We're a mixture of native, indigenous people—the Taino Indians—and African slaves that were brought to the island, as well as Europeans who mingled and intermarried with those people.

My father comes from a family of nine, and within that family they have the full range of possible colors and shades. Some are a light-colored complexion, which is jaundice or high yellow. Some are caramel-colored. And I have an aunt and uncle who are mocha; they're dark.

One day when my father and his siblings were still kids, my grandfather invited an acquaintance to meet the family. So, as was customary, the acquaintance came into the house and was led into the living room, where he took a seat. The children lined up to meet and greet this new guest in my grandfather's house. One by one, they greeted him with a smile and a hug.

But when my aunt and uncle greeted him, he pushed them away. So, they tried again. And he pushed them away. And a third time.

Finally, he turned to my grandfather and said, "Do me a favor. Can you ask the maid's children to leave me alone?" It was suddenly apparent that the man had assumed, because my aunt and uncle had darker skin than others in the lineup, that they weren't members of our family.

My grandfather, who was usually pretty even-keeled, said, "You know what? Do *me* a favor. Get out of my house! Those are *my* children."

I relay that story because there are often situations and circumstances that conspire against us—people who make us feel as though we do not belong in God's family, people who judge us and put a label on us and make us question whether or not we have truly been adopted into God's family. But according to the infallible, inerrant Word of God, if you have surrendered your life to Jesus Christ and have been born again, you are a child of God. You can grow closer to God, and it is your birthright to be led by the Spirit of God. You can have complete assurance that you belong to Him.

You Belong in the Family

The Bible says clearly that if you do not have the Spirit of Christ, you do not belong to Him (see Romans 8:9). In other words, the quality or characteristic that determines whether or not you are a child of God is whether or not you possess within you the life of God through the indwelling Holy Spirit.

How does this happen? When you surrender yourself to Jesus, the Holy Spirit comes to live in you, and He gives you a new life—a God-centered, God-glorifying life.

This has nothing to do with religion or being religious. Probably one of the most religious people Jesus knew during His earthly life was a man named Nicodemus. He was a Pharisee, a meticulously religious leader. He came to Jesus one night in secret, probably to protect his reputation within the religious community, and he seemed to be seeking information from Jesus.

But Jesus cut to the chase: "I tell you the truth, unless you are born again, you cannot see the Kingdom of God" (John 3:3 NLT). Jesus had to reiterate this point several times for Nicodemus, and that very religious man still may not have understood. Religion and religiousness can sometimes obscure more than they enlighten.

Jesus continued, saying that being born on earth got a person into a human family, but that we must be born again to enter God's family.

It is often said that we—all of humanity—are all children of God. You hear it all the time in popular songs, political speeches and so on. But Jesus did not say that all people are children of God. And the Bible does not teach that. It is true that we were all created in the image of God. Every human life has inherent dignity and value. All people are not, however, children of God. That is something different.

This does not mean that God is a hater. He is not; He is a lover. He loves all people. The problem is not that God does not love people, but that people do not love God. John's gospel says:

> For God did not send his Son into the world to condemn the world, but to save the world through him. Whoever believes in him is not condemned, but whoever does not believe stands condemned already because they have not believed in the name of God's one and only Son. This is the verdict: Light has come into the world, but people loved darkness instead of light because their deeds were evil.
>
> John 3:17–19

And to those who receive Him, He gives the Holy Spirit, who brings the assurance that they are not orphans but children of God—full-fledged members of the family (see John 1:12–13).

Scripture confirms this truth of the new birth for us: "Anyone who belongs to Christ has become a new person. The old life is gone; a new life has begun!" (2 Corinthians 5:17 NLT).

The moment you placed your faith in Jesus Christ to save you from sin, guilt and condemnation, "God put his stamp of ownership on you by giving you the Holy Spirit he had promised" (Ephesians 1:13 GNT).

You were baptized into the Body of Christ when you believed. "For we were all baptized by one Spirit so as to form one body—whether Jews or Gentiles, slave or free—and we were all given the one Spirit to drink" (1 Corinthians 12:13). You were submerged into the family of God.

Regardless of where you come from, your socioeconomic status, your ethnicity or the color of your skin, you can know that you are in God's family. He receives people of every shape and size, from all walks of life. It does not matter where you have been or what you have done, because the moment you came to Christ, He gave you a new life through the work of the Holy Spirit.

Did you catch that? It is a *new* life. It is not always easy to understand or fully comprehend. After all, the day I put my faith in Jesus and looked in the mirror, do you know who I saw? Me.

So, is Jesus just fixing up the old me? Making me a better version of me? No. It is more than that. He does not simply patch up my old life. He does not rehabilitate old things. He makes new things. The beauty of adoption is that the moment you are adopted by your new family, your reality completely changes. Whatever existed in the past is in the past. What is most true about you is your new family, and most importantly, who your dad is. It is all new. Not just slightly better. New.

The Holy Spirit's job is to make sure you have, as John Wesley put it, that "inward impression on the soul, whereby the Spirit of God immediately and directly witnesses to my spirit, that I am a child of God; that Jesus Christ hath loved me, and given himself for me; that all my sins are blotted out, and I, even I, am reconciled to God."[2]

Romans 8:16 (NLT) says, "His Spirit joins with our spirit to affirm that we are God's children." Do you know how that happens? Have you ever tried, after you became a follower of Jesus, to hang around with people you used to hang around with? Have you ever tried to go to places that you used to go to, or do things you did before, only to find out that something was not right, that you felt out of place, strange and uncomfortable? Or have you had that surprising experience of saying you are "not a church person," only to find yourself liking church and "those church people"? Do you know what that is? That is His Spirit affirming to your spirit that you are God's child. It is the Holy Spirit letting you know that you are new. You do not belong in the same old places, among the same old crowd, doing the same old things. You are beyond all that. You are a child of God.

The King Is My Dad

In describing the Holy Spirit's work, the Bible also makes it clear that the Spirit engenders within us a supernatural sense of nearness and communion with God. The apostle Paul said, "The Spirit you received does not make you slaves, so that you live in fear again; rather, the Spirit you received brought about your adoption to sonship. And by him we cry, 'Abba, Father'" (Romans 8:15).

We are God's children with all the rights and privileges that come with being full members of the family. The Holy Spirit affirms that we are sons and daughters of God. We tend to forget, so He is right there to remind us when we most need it.

When the Bible says that we cry *Abba*, it uses a precise word. Its equivalent in English could be *Papa* or *Dada*. It is an Aramaic word that echoes the first syllables an infant learns to associate with a loving father. In other cultures and languages, the term might be *Papi* (Spanish), *Baba* (Mandarin), *Appa* (Tamil) or *Bapu* (Indonesian). It is a term of intimacy and endearment.

Some children address their parents more formally than others. A friend I grew up with called her parents *Mother* and *Father*, never anything else. Sometimes, my children might refer to me as their father or address me as *Dad*. But when I answer the phone and hear *Daddy*, my heart melts. It is usually followed by a plea for money, but still. . . .

The Spirit each of us received upon becoming a follower of Jesus puts the word *Abba* in our hearts and in our mouths. Through the Holy Spirit, we relate to God—the immortal, invisible, infinite, eternal God of the ages—as *Abba*. Through the Spirit, we do not relate to Him only as servants or subjects but also as beloved children, as though we crawl into His lap and stroke His face and fall asleep in His arms. The King of all creation is the world's best Dad . . . and we are His kids!

We can say with the psalmist, "Keep me as the apple of your eye" (Psalm 17:8). We can believe in the promise, "He will cover you with his feathers and under his wings you will find refuge" (Psalm 91:4). We can draw near to Him, expecting that He will draw near to us (see James 4:8). Though our God is King of all, we can boldly approach His throne as a child might burst into the royal presence, oblivious to pomp and circumstance, and run into the Father's arms (see Hebrews 4:16). Because of the indwelling Spirit, we can relax and rest, safe in Abba's love, because "perfect love drives out fear" (1 John 4:18).

The Kids Get the Inheritance

In addition to the assurance, guidance and intimacy that come with the Holy Spirit's residence in our lives, He is a pledge concerning our inheritance (see 2 Corinthians 5:5). If you have ever made a large purchase of something you would take possession of later, such as land or a house, you probably had to make an earnest payment—a sizeable sum of money to guarantee that you would not change your mind or renege on your promise.

The Bible says that "the Spirit is God's guarantee that he will give us the inheritance he promised and that he has purchased us to be his own people" (Ephesians 1:14 NLT). God "set his seal of ownership on us, and put his Spirit in our hearts as a deposit, guaranteeing what is to come" (2 Corinthians 1:22).

We have a hope. A future. An inheritance. When this life ends, we do not die: We graduate. The Salvation Army calls it a "promotion to Glory." And the Spirit is not only a deposit guaranteeing "that he who began a good work in you will carry it on to completion until the day of Christ Jesus" (Philippians 1:6); He is also a "foretaste of glory divine."[3] You see, when you make an earnest payment, you give *some* of what will be paid *in full* later on. So, the Holy Spirit's presence in our lives is the same "stuff," so to speak, that will come later, in full, "when completeness comes" (1 Corinthians 13:10). The love, joy, peace, forbearance, kindness, goodness, faithfulness, gentleness and self-control that the Spirit brings into our earthly lives is a taste of the glorified life that is to come. As the carol says, "God imparts to human hearts the blessings of His heaven."[4] He does this through the indwelling Holy Spirit at work in the lives of all who place their trust in Christ and receive His salvation.

FOR REFLECTION

- What tends to make you forget that you are one of God's kids? And when do you most need to be reminded?

SIX

LIVING WITH CLARITY

THEY COULD NOT TELL which way was up. And it cost them their lives.

At 8:39 p.m. on July 16, 1999, a small plane piloted by John F. Kennedy Jr. departed from New Jersey's Essex County Airport. He and his passengers—his wife, Carolyn, and her sister, Lauren— were headed to a family wedding after a stop at Martha's Vineyard. Carolyn had spoken on the phone to a friend before their departure and promised to call when they landed.

That call never came.

At 10:05 p.m., the air traffic controller at Martha's Vineyard Airport instructed an intern to contact the Federal Aviation Administration (FAA) office in Bridgeport, Connecticut, saying that Kennedy's plane had not arrived. Just over four hours later, a Kennedy family member reported the missing plane to the local Coast Guard Air Station. A search-and-rescue operation was launched at 4:00 a.m. on July 17. Fragments of the plane were located two days later, and on July 21, Navy divers recovered the bodies of John F. Kennedy Jr. and his passengers, still strapped into their seats.

Months later, the National Transportation Safety Board completed its investigation and reported that Kennedy's plane had spun into the Atlantic Ocean 7.5 miles off the coast of Martha's Vineyard. The probable cause of the crash was spatial disorientation. That is, they were flying through darkness with a hazy sky overhead, a murky ocean below and a featureless horizon ahead.

The pilot could not tell which way was up.

The courses of our lives are fraught with darkness and danger as we fly through unfriendly skies. We often do not know what to think, where to turn or which way is up. Yet we cannot afford to succumb to "spiritual disorientation." We need help—perhaps far more help than we know—to see clearly through the night that surrounds us and threatens to undo us.

The Holy Spirit Gathers

On the evening that He was arrested, Jesus told His closest friends and followers:

> "When the Helper comes, He will show the world the truth about sin. He will show the world about being right with God. And He will show the world what it is to be guilty. He will show the world about sin, because they do not put their trust in Me. He will show the world about being right with God, because I go to My Father and you will see Me no more. He will show the world what it is to be guilty because the leader of this world (Satan) is guilty. . . . The Holy Spirit is coming. He will lead you into all truth. He will not speak His Own words. He will speak what He hears. He will tell you of things to come. He will honor Me. He will receive what is Mine and will tell it to you. Everything the Father has is Mine. That is why I said to you, 'He will receive what is Mine and will tell it to you.'"
>
> John 16:8–15 NLV

Jesus was pointing out that the Holy Spirit is gathering people to God. At the time, however, His followers had no context for

Jesus' description of the Holy Spirit and His work. In fact, they may have heard very little after Jesus said, "I'm going away."

Say what, Jesus? You're going where? When? What?

We have something of an advantage over those first followers. We encounter His words on the other side of His crucifixion, resurrection and ascension. Our minds and hearts are not muddled by the dread and trauma of the events they endured firsthand. Yet Jesus' words apply as much to us as they did to Peter, James, John and the others.

You think the world is messed up and dark? Imagine that world without the Holy Spirit, without the presence of God gathering people to Him. I hate even to think about the world without the presence of the Holy Spirit. Just as He was the hovering presence over the dark surface of the deep at Creation, He is the holy presence on the earth today, dispelling darkness, being the source of all joy, peace, patience, kindness and gentleness. His gathering efforts take many forms, but we can summarize them in three ways.

The Holy Spirit Convicts

The Holy Spirit is constantly speaking to people, telling them there is a better way than the way they are living, convicting them of sin, saying, "Yes, you are a sinner, like everyone else in the world. Don't you think it's time that you admit it? Confront it? Get some help with it? Be forgiven? Cleansed?"

He does not put people out with the trash; He puts the trash out of people. He does not give up on people; He prompts them to give up their sin. He does not turn His back on people; He turns them back toward the God who loves them and gave His all for them. We can all be thankful that He continues to transform us as followers of Jesus (we will say more about that later).

There are probably people in your family you are concerned about because they do not know Jesus. You worry. You fret. You strategize. You might even preach and pester them. But the Holy

Spirit is doing far more work than you know—far more than you will ever do to get them to come to Jesus. The Holy Spirit puts them on your heart and you pray for them, but your job is not to convict them of sin. That is the Holy Spirit's job.

R. A. Torrey, a famous preacher and author, wrote:

> We are very sharp-sighted as regards the sins and shortcomings of others, but very blind to our own. And the world is so blind to its sinfulness that no one but the Holy Spirit can ever convince the world of sin, that is, can ever bring [men and women] to see how sinful they are. No matter how great our natural powers of reasoning and persuasion may be, we cannot produce real conviction of sin by all our arguments and all our pathetic stories. We can get [people] to cry by telling pathetic stories (and by singing songs about "Tell Mother I'll Be There"), but *mere shedding of tears over pathetic stories and touching songs is not conviction of sin. Real conviction of sin can only be produced by the Holy Spirit.*[1]

You cannot do the Spirit's work for Him, but you can be used by Him in the process. Nineteenth-century evangelist Charles Finney once entered a factory near Utica, New York. He saw some of the young women watching him while they worked, talking and laughing together. Saying nothing, he approached them. When he stood about ten feet away, one of the women "was quite overcome, and sunk down, and burst into tears. The impression caught like powder, and in a few moments nearly all in the room were in tears."[2]

The owner of the factory saw this and stopped the machines. A prayer meeting ensued, and a revival spread for days through that factory.

This part of the Spirit's work continues in a person's life even after he or she experiences new life in Christ. Do you know why it bothers you when you sin? Do you know why thoughts and behaviors that never concerned you before disturb you now? It is not because you are good. It is not because you are super-spiritual. It is because the Holy Spirit is in your life, and He shines light into darkness and convicts you of your sin. Indeed, he convicts all people of their sin.

Conviction is wonderful. It is better than condemnation because conviction always provides a way out. Condemnation drives us further from God, but the Holy Spirit convicts in order to draw us closer to God. Condemnation produces fear, but conviction points us toward forgiveness. Condemnation leads only to guilt and shame, but conviction, if it leads to repentance, opens the door to grace and glory.

The Holy Spirit Calls

In His late-night conversation with Nicodemus, Jesus compared the Holy Spirit to the wind. It was an easy play on words, since in Hebrew, Aramaic and Greek, the word is the same. He said, "The Spirit is like the wind that blows wherever it wants to. You can hear the wind, but you don't know where it comes from or where it is going" (John 3:8 CEV).

The Holy Spirit is invisible, but He is not inaudible. He speaks. He calls. He cajoles and courts and coaxes.

I am the youngest of five kids in my family. My brother is eight years older, and there are three sisters between us. So, when I was in the fourth grade, my brother was getting ready to graduate from high school and go into the Air Force.

And I was happy to see him go. I was young and did not know much about him at all. Here is what I did know: He got into a lot of trouble, and that meant unpleasant interactions with our dad. I was glad when he left because the house felt more peaceful and less scary to this young boy with him gone. But then my brother met Jesus in the Air Force. He would call home and tell us he had become what he was calling a "born again" Christian. I had no idea what that meant.

When I was a freshman in high school, my brother invited me to go to a Christian music festival called Fishnet. I did not know what that was. I did not even know there was such a thing as Christian music. I just knew it would be awesome to travel in an RV with a bunch of Air Force guys. And I wanted to get to know my brother. What happened over those few days changed my life. It was not a sermon. It was not some big moment. It was the look in their eyes—thousands of people there with that look in their eyes like they knew something I did not, like they knew God on a personal level and it mattered to them in a very real, everyday kind of way.

I remember sitting on the grass while one of the bands played. A banner hung over the stage that said, "Lord of All." Thousands of people all around me were sitting and smiling and enjoying the concert, but something else was going on inside me, something invisible. Even the people sitting right next to me did not know it. It felt as if I was thinking these strange thoughts, but now I know that I was praying. I finally said, *God, if what these people know is You, then I want to get to know You.*

That was it. I never even spoke the words out loud.

When I got back home to New Jersey, I looked in the Yellow Pages for the kind of church my brother was going to. (These were the B.G. days—"Before Google.") I found the closest one to my house and asked my mother if she would drive me there on Sunday. Not knowing anything about church except the Catholic Masses of my childhood, I was unsure what to expect. My family had become nonpracticing Catholics, so, as I look back, I have to give my mom a ton of credit for driving me to this unknown church. (Way to go, Mom!)

I began to learn and grow in that church. I met the youth pastor and he helped me tremendously. I got baptized. And now, thirty years later, I have spent my entire adult life serving as a pastor in the local church. Who would have imagined such a thing?

Now, if you asked me about the exact moment when I got saved, was born again, became a Christian or surrendered my life to Jesus, I am not sure I could answer precisely. It was a process, all of it orchestrated by the Holy Spirit. To this day, whenever I am back in New Jersey and drive by Nassau Christian Center in Princeton, a flood of good memories comes to mind from that season of my life.

Do you remember how God gathered you to Himself? Do you remember the process? Perhaps people were praying for you, someone said something or you were invited somewhere. Maybe you were the recipient of an act of kindness. Or maybe you were going through a tough season and started thinking that there must be a better way to live. For others, it began with the realization of a need for forgiveness. It is entirely possible that picking up and reading this book is part of the process for some. Many people I have met say that there was simply and unexplainably an increased and surprising interest in the things of God.

But it can be explained: The Holy Spirit calls.

Do you remember the process? Do you remember when you first started thinking, *Maybe I'll do that. Maybe I'll go to church. Maybe I'll have the conversation.* Can you pinpoint where it started? God put someone in your path. The Holy Spirit orchestrated a series of events, and you were probably unaware of it all until fairly late in the process. Am I right? I bet I am. The gathering process began—whispering, poking, persuading, breaking, convicting—long before the Spirit captured your heart.

The Holy Spirit Captures

At our church we have regular newcomers' receptions where we invite new attendees to enjoy free food, meet the pastors and ask questions. I cannot tell you how often I hear something like what one guy told me recently. He said, "I haven't been in church in, like, . . . thirty years. It's not really like me to be standing here talking to a preacher, but I just . . ."

He could not find the words.

"Man, there's something going on, and I just want . . ."

I smiled and nodded, because I knew exactly what he was going through. I said something profound like, "Well, just keep coming back."

But I could have said, "Man, you're getting captured by the Gatherer. Man, brace yourself. Your whole life's about to change in an awesome, glorious, wonderful way. God has His eyes on you. The Spirit has His hand on you. And you're getting captured."

I love seeing that; it is often surprising and always amazing. I have watched people in my family who were—how do I say this?—hard cases. You may have somebody in your family like that—someone who makes you think, *Yeah, that one will* never *follow Jesus.* And then it happens, and you just shake your head because you never thought that one would get captured, but all along, the Holy Spirit was doing far more work for far longer than you ever knew.

The Holy Spirit Guides

Not only does the Holy Spirit gather, but He also guides, and He guides by His voice. This world and age in which we live can be so confusing and daunting, disorienting and dangerous. Without the Spirit's guidance, we could easily lose our bearings. That is why Jesus promised a Helper who "will lead you into all truth. He will not speak His Own words. He will speak what He hears. He will tell you of things to come" (John 16:13 NLV).

This may be hard for young people to believe, but we have not always had GPSs in our cars or on our phones. Back in the day, we did not have satellites telling us where to go. We had to rely on a voice from the passenger seat saying, "Turn left. Slow down. Why are you going this way?" It was the person holding the map.

But these days, we have wonderful turn-by-turn navigation that will get you anywhere—if you enter the right information. Nobody wants to put in the wrong address and end up driving three hours for a pizza. The app I use shows me road construction ahead and will reroute my path if traffic patterns change. It will even tell me where the police are. (Not that I need that. I just use that feature to pray for them and bless them in Jesus' name. Honest!)

The Holy Spirit is like that—an inner guide, a spiritual GPS. If you are just beginning in your walk with Jesus, you might not know that you have a Guide living inside you. He is not only a conscience—convicting of sin, showing you right from wrong, telling you when you are safe or in danger—He is also a coach, telling you to run faster and work smarter until you reach your goals. He is the Person sitting beside you with the map, saying, "Slow down. Turn left. Why are you going this way?"

I would never want to try to serve Jesus without this Coach, Helper and Guide. And you, too, can grow in this awareness of the Holy Spirit guiding and leading you.

Jesus told His followers:

> On my account you will be brought before governors and kings as witnesses to them and to the Gentiles. But when they arrest you, do not worry about what to say or how to say it. At that time you will be given what to say, for it will not be you speaking, but the Spirit of your Father speaking through you.
>
> Matthew 10:18–20

Now, I have never been arrested and forced to explain myself to a governor or a king. But I have experienced the quality of the Holy Spirit that Jesus promised in this verse. It has been fulfilled in my life over and over again.

God is always speaking, and the Holy Spirit's work is to translate (and sometimes amplify) the voice of God to the child of God. Our problem is not that God does not speak, but that we are not always listening. So, here is the key question: How do we learn to hear the voice of God? When other people say, "God told me," or

"The Spirit urged me," do you wonder if they have some kind of direct phone line to God that you were not given? They seem to have a Snapchat streak going with God, while we can barely get Him to reply to a text!

Then the comparisons start in our minds. They are better; we are worse. They are spiritual; we are worldly. Right? Wrong!

All followers of Jesus can learn to hear the voice of God. The question is not *if* we can hear Him, but *how*. How do we learn to hear the voice of God?

The answer is easy: With our feet!

Our ability to hear the Spirit's voice is sharpened through obedience. Jesus said, "Those who accept my commandments and obey them are the ones who love me. And because they love me, my Father will love them. And I will love them and reveal myself to each of them" (John 14:21 NLT).

Our obedience aids the Spirit's work in our lives so that the more we obey, the more we hear. Just as when the children of Israel were preparing to cross the Jordan River into the Promised Land, God will not reveal the next step to us if we have ignored the previous step He told us to take.

As we hear and obey the things God has already told us, following the ways in which He has already led us, God reveals the next step to us.

Let's say, for instance, you are having issues in your family—maybe with a child or member of your extended family—and God may be saying, "Apologize."

That is not easy to hear, but when you obey, He reveals more. He may say, "Now, wait before speaking further to that person."

So you wait.

And then, maybe He gives a nudge that the other person is ready to talk further, so you go to that person and things happen that you could never have engineered without being led by the Spirit of God—things that "No eye has seen, no ear has heard, and no mind has imagined" (1 Corinthians 2:9 NLT).

How else does the Spirit guide us? He leads sometimes by pointing to Scripture. Have you ever been in a situation where a verse you did not even know you knew suddenly springs to mind? That is the Holy Spirit at work.

Suppose, for instance, that I mess up, cross the line with my wife and get . . . *the look*. You know the look? It means *You mere mortal man*. It is in that moment that I want the Holy Spirit to remind her of the first commandment of marriage: "Thou shalt not kill" (Exodus 20:13 KJV).

See how that works? The answer is not simply hearing God; a fancy set of spiritual hearing aids will not help if we are not acting on what He is saying. If we want to hear more from God, we need to give Him a reason to tell us more.

I think this is one of the most fun things about being a Christian. God speaks, and although we do not fully understand the why, what or how of what He is asking us to do—we may not even be one-hundred-percent sure He even spoke—we do our best to walk it out in simple obedience. And what happens? Sometimes we see the results, which is almost always exhilarating or encouraging. Other times, though, we do not see the results. It sometimes feels as though the results are shared on a need-to-know basis, and God does not seem to think we need to know. Even then, however, we get the inner assurance and satisfaction of an accomplished assignment, and that can be enormously satisfying.

This never gets old to me. It pushes me out of my comfort zone, challenges me to trust and reminds me that God is always up to something. As we say often in our church: He is on a redeeming, restoring and reconciling mission.

The Holy Spirit also leads us subjectively through what Wesley called an "inward impression." You may remember a simple grade school experiment in which salt was sprinkled onto a drumhead or similar surface and music was played nearby, causing the salt granules to move on the surface in response to the sound vibrations.

Something similar happens in the soul that is indwelt by the Holy Spirit. The Spirit resonates with the sound of the Shepherd's voice (see John 10:27) and translates every pulse and pitch for the receptive soul. And He adjusts the frequency, so to speak, to every waiting heart. My wife told me once that God does not talk to her the way He talks to me. That is true. He does not talk to her the way He talks to me, but He does talk to her . . . and to you. He talks to each of us on our own frequency.

Have you ever felt that God might be telling you to do something? Our friend and fellow pastor, Raul Latoni, helps with an illustration:

> On one occasion, there was an older couple at church that liked me a lot, for some reason. They gave me a card on my birthday, and inside was a nice, crisp hundred-dollar bill. I don't see a lot of hundred-dollar bills, so this was pretty exciting. I immediately started making plans for how I would spend it.
>
> There's this restaurant called Texas Roadhouse. They have a twenty-ounce Porterhouse steak. I love steak. And I was thinking I would get a medium rare Porterhouse, baked sweet yams, all the trimmings. Oh yes! And then, suddenly, God spoke to my heart: *That's not for you.*
>
> I can't describe the voice, but it was clear and definite. I knew I needed to give that nice, crisp hundred-dollar bill to someone else.
>
> There was another pastor in the church, so I went to him, gave him the hundred-dollar bill, and said, "Listen, I believe in your ministry, and I'm glad that you're here. I think the Lord told me to give you this."
>
> Now, believe me, that wasn't me. I am not that good. I like steak so much, I would much rather have said, "This is the spirit of poverty. Get thee behind me, Satan. Let's go eat some steak."
>
> But I knew better. I am a child of God, and I would rather be led by the Spirit of God than by my own cravings for slightly cooked meat.

The Bible says, "Those who are led by the Spirit of God are the children of God" (Romans 8:14). If you ever wonder whether it is your voice or the voice of others you are hearing instead of God's leading, there is one reliable way to figure that out. If you are feeling led to do something selfless, perhaps something for someone other than yourself, it is probably the Spirit of God. Why? Because few of us are that good and generous all on our own. The Spirit will not lead us back into our old tendencies. Instead, He will repeatedly call us forward into better ways and higher purposes than we are naturally inclined to go. He is not likely to lead us to approach someone in the grocery store and say, "God just told me that you should give me money."

But if you feel a strong urge to give, to be generous, kind, compassionate, helpful and attentive to someone else, there is a good chance that it is the Spirit speaking to you.

Have you had this happen? You are dealing with a situation, and you have no idea what you are going to do or say, but you think, *Lord, I know You're going to go with me.* Then you go into that situation and hear yourself saying things that are more brilliant than you ever dreamed. You start thinking, *Wow! That was good! I need to write that down so I don't forget it.*

Chances are, that was the Holy Spirit giving you the wisdom and the words. It might even be an unfair advantage in business if you have the Holy Spirit and the people around you do not, because sometimes the Holy Spirit goes before you and gives you insight: *Here's what's really going on beneath the surface. Here's why this employee is struggling. Here's what you can say to these clients.*

If you are a parent responding to a situation with your kids, and later you think to yourself, *Where did that come from?* it might be the Spirit. If you are in ministry of some kind, and you respond to a challenge better than you thought you were capable of doing, it was probably the Spirit.

About twenty years ago I was leading a youth ministry, and one particular student was giving me trouble. So, I arranged a meeting with his parents. Unfortunately, the parents did not seem to care too much for me—hard to imagine, I know—and I did not really like their kid that much either, to be honest. I loved him in Jesus' name and wanted the best for him, I just thought it would be best for him to be far away from me.

I spoke to the mom about her son's behavior, and she said, "Well, you have a lot of silly little rules in your youth ministry."

I heard the words coming from her mouth, but I found them hard to believe. I had no idea how to respond. Finally, I opened my mouth, and these are the words that came out: "If the rules are silly and little, then your child should have no problem following them."

As soon as I said that, I thought, *Hang on. I've got to write that down.* It was the perfect response in that situation. It was so good, I knew it had not come from me. I am not that smart. Smart *aleck*, yes. But smart, no. It was just the wisdom I needed at that moment, and that kid and I functioned together much better after that meeting. I believe the wisdom came from the Holy Spirit, who lives in me and guides me.

As He guides us, we learn to recognize and follow His promptings. We might get it wrong from time to time, but even then, what father does not love it when his children try to listen and obey? Can you imagine?

"Dad, I wanted to please you, so I took the trash out to the curb without you asking me fourteen thousand times."

You smile and say "Thank you," even if trash day was yesterday. It still counts.

If you are listening for the Spirit's voice, He will be pleased by your attempts. He does not expect perfection, but He will respond to sincere effort. *Is that You, Holy Spirit? Am I hearing You right? I hope I'm hearing what You're saying.* Especially when the instruction you think you hear stretches you a little:

Shovel your neighbor's driveway for her.

"Yes, Lord."

Tip a little extra to your server, even though she never refilled your coffee cup.

"If You say so, Lord."

Get off the couch and apologize to your spouse.

"Really, Lord? Okay, yes."

When the Holy Spirit comes into your life, He imparts a supernatural ability to be led by Him. The Bible says, "Those who are led by the Spirit of God are the children of God" (Romans 8:14). Being led by the Spirit of God is a mark of your family relationship. It is your birthright as a child of God to hear His Spirit's voice, to be led by Him and to be given supernatural wisdom to fly the unfriendly skies of this life.

That is why every time you open Scripture there is an affirmation, an "amen" on the inside. If you are like me, you do not pray for intellectual knowledge. You do not look for mere entertainment or education. Instead, you pray, "Holy Spirit, show me what You want me to know and what You want me to see. I want to know You better. I plan to hear and obey Your voice. And as You show me what You want me to see and hear, I'm going to grow and You're going to help me. It's going to encourage me. It's going to strengthen me. You're going to lead me and guide me."

The more you read His words, the better you will get at recognizing and heeding His voice. The more you ask, the more He will answer. And the more you obey, the more He will lead.

The Holy Spirit Glorifies Jesus

The Holy Spirit gathers. The Holy Spirit guides. And the Holy Spirit glorifies Jesus. Always.

Jesus told His followers, "The Holy Spirit is coming. . . . He will honor Me. He will receive what is Mine and will tell it to you" (John 16:13–14 NLV).

The Holy Spirit glorifies Jesus. This is a beautiful thing. It can help us recognize when we are being led by the Spirit.

Christian preacher and author J. I. Packer explained it this way:

> When floodlighting is well done, the floodlights are so placed that you do not see them; you are not in fact supposed to see where the light is coming from; what you are meant to see is just the building on which the floodlights are trained. The intended effect is to make it visible when otherwise it would not be seen for the darkness, and to maximize its dignity by throwing all its details into relief so that you see it properly. This perfectly illustrates the Spirit's new covenant role. He is, so to speak, the hidden floodlight shining on the Saviour.
>
> Or think of it this way. It is as if the Spirit stands behind us, throwing light over our shoulder, on Jesus, who stands facing us. The Spirit's message to us is never, "Look at me; listen to me; come to me; get to know me," but always, "Look at him, and see his glory; listen to him, and hear his word; go to him, and have life; get to know him, and taste his gift of joy and peace." The Spirit, we might say, is the matchmaker, the celestial marriage broker, whose role it is to bring us and Christ together and ensure that we stay together.[3]

I am fascinated by the humility and deference that exists within the Trinity. Paul wrote:

> Have the same mindset as Christ Jesus: Who, being in very nature God, did not consider equality with God something to be used to his own advantage; rather, he made himself nothing by taking the very nature of a servant, being made in human likeness. And being found in appearance as a man, he humbled himself by becoming obedient to death—even death on a cross!
>
> Philippians 2:5–8

And because He was willing to do that, what did the Father do?

Therefore God exalted him to the highest place and gave him the name that is above every name, that at the name of Jesus every knee should bow, in heaven and on earth and under the earth, and every tongue acknowledge that Jesus Christ is Lord, to the glory of God the Father.

Philippians 2:9–11

The Son humbles Himself. The Father exalts the Son. The Son's triumph glorifies the Father. The Spirit honors the Son. And on and on it goes. I love this about the Trinity. It is a perfect picture of corporate humility that the people of God are called to reflect as Christ's Body.

And that attitude then becomes a reflection of the Holy Spirit's presence in us to use everything—every blessing, every gift, every advantage we enjoy—to glorify God and point to Jesus.

I had dinner recently with a friend who had been in local government, held a position of some authority and later retired. I asked, "How's retirement? How's it going? How are you doing? What do you miss?"

He described some things about the job he did not miss. But he said he desperately missed the ability to influence individual lives. He told me stories and got emotional about times when he had touched individual lives and ministered to people. Now in retirement, however, he is finding blessing after blessing from getting involved in the healing center at our church, where we offer practical, social and spiritual support to individuals and families in need.

Why would he do that? Why not just spend all his time golfing or parasailing or watching television? Because the Holy Spirit is inside him, looking for a way to leverage his many gifts and abilities to glorify God and point to Jesus.

That is evidence of the Holy Spirit's presence in a person's life—the desire to glorify Jesus. The Spirit *always* seeks to glorify Jesus. If you read the gospels, you know that Jesus is always saying, "Have you met My Father?" And the Father is always showing up just to brag on His Son. "Here's My Son! I'm so pleased with Him." Then He pulls out His smartphone and starts showing pictures.

That is how the Holy Spirit operates. He gathers. He guides. And He glorifies Jesus, pointing the way to Him. When the Spirit lives in us, our lives become more and more a reflection of the Holy Spirit's life—gathering people who need the Lord, being guided by His voice in all we do, glorifying God and pointing to Jesus.

FOR REFLECTION

- How have you personally experienced the gathering, guiding and glorifying work of the Holy Spirit?

- What does "hearing with your feet" mean to you?

SEVEN

LIVING IN GOOD COMPANY

THE NEIGHBORHOOD surrounding my family's house on Kellogg Street in Bethel, Connecticut, seemed at the time to be the ultimate kids' neighborhood.

I lived there from my first-grade year through fourth grade, and in my memory every house had kids in it, ranging from preschool age all the way through high school. We were always outside—playing in backyards, in the woods, at the pond, or around the lake. I am sure our parents did not always know where we were, but we were always among friends, so if something happened, any one of us could have run to get help.

In those days there were no cell phones, of course, but my mom employed a sophisticated communications device—an enormous cowbell to tell us that it was time to come home. She would step out on the back porch and ring the cowbell. The sound seemed to carry through the air all the way to Hartford or Long Island.

One day, having heard the bell, my friends and I split up, each to his own house. I pedaled my bike toward home. On the way, however, was a spot by the side of the road where someone had created two dirt bike ramps—a little one for younger kids and a larger one for older kids. The large ramp had a pit after it so you had to make sure you jumped high enough to clear the pit before landing.

On this day, I finally felt brave enough to try the larger ramp. I started my run as far back as I could and pedaled harder than I ever had before. I hit the ramp at top speed and launched into the air. I braced for the impact on the other side of the pit, but my rear tire clipped the edge of the pit and I crashed. I soared over the handlebars and landed hard, my head slamming against the ground. My breath was knocked out of me. I could not move. I was hurting. And I was alone, lying on the ground, afraid. I could not tell if I had broken bones or if I had seriously injured myself. I just knew I needed help and there was none to be found. I do not know how long it took me to stand up, but eventually I got up and walked my bike home. I cried the entire way, but I knew I had to make it because home was where the help was.

Perhaps you have had a similar experience. Maybe you were separated from your parents in a busy shopping center and experienced the sensation of being suddenly and frighteningly alone. Or you may have waited for someone to pick you up from school and worried about being forgotten. Such acute feelings of aloneness can even afflict us in adulthood—your first night in a college dorm room, for example, or that time you were stranded in a strange city, or when you had to say good-bye to your dearest friend.

Do you remember how that felt? How intense, even traumatic that feeling was? Jesus knows that feeling. In fact, He prepared His closest friends and followers for His arrest, crucifixion, burial and ascension by saying, "I will not leave you as orphans" (John 14:18).

When He said that, was He remembering the death of His earthly father, Joseph? (It seems to have taken place sometime between Jesus' bar mitzvah and the beginning of His public ministry.) Did He fasten His gaze on one or two of His disciples as

He said those words, addressing the men that He knew would be most upset by His warning that "before long, the world will not see me anymore" (John 14:19)?

We cannot know, of course, but we do know that Jesus promised never to leave His disciples alone. Further, by sending the Holy Spirit, He ensured that they would never be abandoned. The Spirit would not only live in them and work through them but also be the blessing of a constant companion and prayer partner.

It is a blessing that Jesus also gives to us.

The Spirit Prays for Us

Have you ever asked a friend to pray for you? Why? Was it because you thought that friend was closer to God than you were? Was it because you believed God would hear two people praying better than He would just one? Was it because you needed someone to help carry your prayer burden?

There are many good reasons for followers of Jesus to pray with, and for, each other. The Bible commands it, for one thing (see 1 Timothy 2:1; Ephesians 6:18). For another, it follows the example of Jesus Himself, who asked His friends to pray with Him (see Matthew 26:38).

Praying together is a way of carrying each other's burdens (see Galatians 6:2) and building stronger and deeper relationships. But did you know that you never pray alone? Whether you have one prayer partner or a prayer chain of hundreds, the Holy Spirit is always praying for you. The Bible says:

> The Spirit helps us in our weakness. We do not know what we ought to pray for, but the Spirit himself intercedes for us through wordless groans. And he who searches our hearts knows the mind of the Spirit, because the Spirit intercedes for God's people in accordance with the will of God.
>
> Romans 8:26–27

Those short verses tell us four immensely important, comforting and breathtaking things about the Spirit:

1. The Spirit helps us in our weakness.

What is your weakness? Are you not sure how to pray? Not sure what to pray? Not very good at it? Too easily distracted? Weak in faith? Weary? Busy?

Whatever your weakness, the Holy Spirit helps you in your weakness. Where you are weak, He is strong. When you are faithless, He is faithful. What you do not know, He knows. He is not hindered by your humanness, discouraged by your defects or frustrated by your lack of faith. He knows you. He knows your inadequacy, and He is available to help you overcome every weakness.

2. The Spirit intercedes for us.

Jesus promised "another advocate" to His followers (see John 14:16). An advocate is a supporter, backer, sponsor—someone who has your interests at heart and speaks on your behalf. So, in addition to Jesus, who "is at the right hand of God and is also interceding for us" (Romans 8:34), we have "the Spirit himself [who] intercedes for us" (Romans 8:26). Whether you pray eloquently or incoherently, "the Spirit of grace and of supplication" (Zechariah 12:10 NASB) stands up for you and speaks out for you. He intercedes for you and for every need you have, no matter what you are thinking, how you feel or where you are.

3. The Spirit prays passionately for us.

The Bible says that the Spirit "intercedes for us through wordless groans" (Romans 8:26). Another translation says, "groanings too deep for words" (Romans 8:26 ESV).

Take a moment to stop and think about that. Why would the Spirit of God groan? It cannot be from exertion like a man trying to lift a heavy load. Nothing is too hard for Him (see Jeremiah 32:27). It cannot be from weariness like an exhausted mom dropping into a chair at the end of the day. He never grows weary (see Isaiah 40:28). Neither is it a groan of pain, frustration or despair.

The Holy Spirit's "wordless groans" come from His amazing love for us and His passionate commitment to us (see 2 Kings 19:31 NLT; Isaiah 9:7; 37:32 NLT), which He pours out "in a breathing and a being that is deeper than utterance."[1]

4. The Spirit prays in accordance with God's will.

You have probably heard people ask for something in prayer and then add *if it be Thy will*. There is nothing wrong about praying that way; it can be a helpful reminder that we do not always know "what we ought to pray for" (Romans 8:26). And just because we think it is a good idea does not mean God ought to do it.

But the Holy Spirit never prays that way, because "he who searches our hearts"—that is, the Father—"knows the mind of the Spirit," and the Spirit always "intercedes for God's people in accordance with the will of God" (Romans 8:27). Father, Son and Holy Spirit think, speak and act in harmony, so the Spirit's passionate intercession for us always aligns with God's will and, thus, promotes the best possible outcome for us. His requests for us are always plan *A*. They are always first class. Always platinum level.

The Spirit Prays with Us

Not only does the Spirit pray *for* us, but He prays *with* us. In fact, the Spirit initiated our intimacy with the Father. The Bible says, "The Spirit you received brought about your adoption to sonship. And by him we cry, 'Abba, Father'" (Romans 8:15). It is the Spirit in our hearts who repeatedly cries out to God with us. "God sent the Spirit of his Son into our hearts, the Spirit who calls out, 'Abba, Father'" (Galatians 4:6).

Whenever we start to pray, regardless of how determined or focused we are, the Holy Spirit prays with us. As followers of Jesus, we never pray alone. The Spirit is always praying with us. In fact, it is the Spirit who makes us want to pray in the first place. He prompts us to think of praying, leads us to prayer and inspires our prayers from beginning to end—from "Our Father . . ." to "Amen." He instructs and corrects us in prayer. He hints and suggests prayers to us, sometimes focusing our thoughts and polishing our words, and at other times making sense when all we have are tears, grunts or stammers.

I am learning to rely on the Holy Spirit's partnership in prayer. If I have neglected prayer for a while (yes—it happens to pastors, too!), I might say, "Holy Spirit, turn my heart back to prayer; help me want to pray again."

If I am in a situation where I am asked to pray, I might quietly ask for His help: "Please give me the thoughts and words to pray right now." Or sometimes even, "Holy Spirit, help me remember her name as I pray for this person." Incidentally, when there is a prayer need and a pastor is present, he or she is always going to be asked to pray. (Not that I am complaining, just that it is predictable.)

At times, I might be overburdened about something and barely able to form thoughts, let alone words, so I might say something like, "Holy Spirit, I don't know what to pray; I need You to fill in the blanks."

Or if I am tempted to pray selfishly, telling God what I want and how I think He ought to answer, I might say, "Holy Spirit, help me in my weakness. Even as I pray these things, I thank You that You intercede for God's people in accordance with the will of God. Change my will and make my heart like a stream of water in Your hand; turn it wherever You will."

The Holy Spirit will never allow us to neglect our prayer lives. You can count on Him to remind you to pray and to be right there praying with you.

After all, He is within you.

The Spirit Prays in Us

Because the Spirit is in us, He prays in and through us, and we are able to "pray in the Spirit on all occasions with all kinds of prayers and requests" (Ephesians 6:18).

What does it mean to "pray in the Spirit"? Is it something different from what we have already discovered? Is it a mystical experience? Is it a practice that only extremely spiritual people can achieve? Or is it possible for all of us?

Let me give you an example. Lately, I have been using a personal trainer to help me get back in shape. I am grateful for his help. He provides direction, encouragement and confidence. His ongoing direction and corrections—"Watch your posture; careful you don't let your elbow go that far out; don't worry about working harder, just stick to the routine"—get great results. It was a bit embarrassing when I first started working with the trainer because I had neglected my physical fitness for such a long time.

How did I let things get so bad?

Have you ever felt that way in your prayer life? Most Christians have, at one time or another. You are not alone in that. What my trainer does for me physically, the Holy Spirit does spiritually. He is good at providing direction as we pray. We just have to admit that we do not know exactly what to do. We want to pray, just as I wanted to get back in good physical shape, but we need help.

Sometimes I walk around our church campus and pray for the church. I usually begin by praying for things of which I am aware. Then at some point during the walk I find myself surprised at the kinds of things I pray—things that were not on my agenda when the prayer walk began and so would not naturally come to mind. That is when I remember that the Holy Spirit, my personal prayer trainer, is right there on the walk with me.

Many followers of Jesus find great blessing by praying in an unknown language, a prayer language that is a gift[2] from God (see 1 Corinthians 12:10) and the meaning of which is known only to

Him. Our church staff encourages the use of this gift, considering it an important tool in the prayer toolbox.

On the other hand, the apostle Paul said, "I will pray with my spirit, but I will also pray with my understanding; I will sing with my spirit, but I will also sing with my understanding" (1 Corinthians 14:15). Jesus prayed "in the Spirit" when He prayed (presumably in Aramaic) outside the tomb of Lazarus, no less than when He prayed alone in the Garden of Gethsemane, saying, "May your will be done" (Matthew 26:42).

This tells us that "praying in the Spirit" can be both intelligible and unintelligible. It is supernatural, and it is sometimes a mystical, mountaintop, moving experience—but it does not have to be. It is not the emotions, words or language that defines "praying in the Spirit" but, rather, our hearts, minds, agendas and priorities aligning with the will of God and the work of the Holy Spirit. Twentieth-century evangelist and author Samuel Logan Brengle wrote:

> It is the work of the Holy Spirit, with our cooperation and glad consent, to search and destroy selfishness out of our hearts and fill them with pure love for God and others. And when this is done we shall not then be asking selfishly, to please ourselves and gratify our appetites, pride, ambition, ease, or vanity (see James 4:3). We shall seek only our Lord's glory and the common good of our fellow human beings, in which, as coworkers and partners, we shall have a common share.
>
> If we ask for success, it is not that we may be exalted but that God may be glorified, that Jesus may secure the purchase of His blood, that others may be saved, and that the kingdom of heaven be established upon earth. If we ask for daily bread, it is not that we may be full but that we may be fitted for daily duty. If we ask for health, it is not only that we may be free from pain and filled with physical comfort but that we may be spent "in publishing the sinner's Friend," in fulfilling the work for which God has placed us here.[3]

A. W. Tozer suggested that "praying in the Spirit" is a matter of "who is doing the praying—our determined hearts or the Holy Spirit?" He goes on: "If the prayer originates with the Holy Spirit, then the wrestling can be beautiful and wonderful; but if we are the victims of our own overheated desires, our praying can be as carnal as any other act."[4]

Jesus did not leave us as orphans. We never pray alone. The Holy Spirit, who lives in us, prays for us. He prays with us, and we pray in Him. His presence and power can take us to a new place in prayer—and in life. It is a place that is not dependent on ourselves: not on our own intelligence, knowledge, eloquence, age, maturity or anything else that we possess apart from Him.

In the Person of the Holy Spirit, we have the perfect prayer partner. We can live in good company, in constant communion with the Father to whom we pray, the Son in whose name we pray and the Spirit who prays for us, with us and in us—and us in Him.

FOR REFLECTION

- In what ways do you need the Holy Spirit to help you to pray?

- How does it change the way you think about praying to know that the Holy Spirit is right there praying with you and for you?

EIGHT

GROWING MORE LIKE THE PERSON GOD CREATED YOU TO BE

WHEN I WAS 24 YEARS OLD, I surrendered my life to Jesus after having run from Him for years. I remember well the sense of relief, reconciliation with God, forgiveness, peace, joy and thankfulness I felt at the time.

And I have lived happily ever after since that time.

You laughed, didn't you? Because you know that is far from true.

As a matter of fact, I was frustrated. Not always, but a lot of the time. You see, when I gave my life to Jesus, He changed things on the inside. I could tell that my desires were changing. I knew that the direction of my life was changing. But I was also aware that I still had the ability to sin. You probably have no idea what I am talking about, right? Except . . . I think you do.

I thought I would be better off as a Christian. I thought I was going to have superhero power. But instead, it was as if there was a part of me that got saved and another part of me that said, "So what? Big deal."

Looking back now, it is obvious that I was naïve—delusional, even—but it is what I thought at the time.

Now that I have grown a bit, I realize that before I surrendered to Jesus, I had a fully developed sinful nature. It knew exactly what to do and how to boss me around. It was in the driver's seat of my life. And then, one day, I surrendered my life to God. The Spirit of God came to me, made me alive to Him and got in the car with me.

The old part of me had something to say about that, because the next day, when I wanted to do freaky things like worship and read Scripture and go to church, the old part of me was not happy: *What are we doing in church?* My mind reeled. *What are you reading? The Bible?* My old sinful nature was crying out, *Not so fast with this Jesus stuff!*

It was like the time my wife and I set off on a trip. I was driving and grew uncomfortably warm, so I thought I would take off my jacket. I saw no reason to stop the car to do this. We would lose precious time.

So, while flying down the highway, I asked my wife, "Hey, would you take the wheel for a second?"

Now, I am not saying this was a good idea. It is probably illegal as well. (I just hope the statute of limitations has run out on this crime.) Note: Do not try this at home (or away from home).

She reached over to take the steering wheel, and I started to peel off my jacket. Suddenly, I heard *wah-wah-wah-wah-wah.* Do you know that sound I am talking about: *wah-wah?* It is the sound of tires hitting those grooves sometimes carved into the side of the road to give warning that your car is veering off course, such as when you are falling asleep . . . or when your wife is supposed to have the wheel.

I wrested one arm free from my jacket, grabbed the steering wheel and screamed, "We're running off the road!"

"Oh," she said calmly. "I forgot I had that."

My mind searched in vain for logic in those words. *You forgot that you were supposed to be holding the wheel that controls our lives right now? You forgot?*

But my voice was calm, even gracious, as I reconsidered ever again handing over possession of the steering wheel, or the TV remote, for that matter.

I said, "That's okay, Honey. Don't worry. We survived."

That is some of what I felt as a young follower of Jesus, as someone who was new to life in the Spirit. I had turned over the wheel to Him, and I wanted the Spirit of God just to take total control of the driving. I wanted to think, now that I was "alive to God in Christ Jesus" (Romans 6:11), that the good would always surface, always steer. But it did not happen that way.

It was as if something rebellious in me was saying, "You've trained us all these years to do whatever we want to do. We're determined to go and do what we've always done."

And I realized I was in a struggle. I wanted this Christian life to be easier. I think I knew I was supposed to fight the devil and the world, but I did not realize that I also had an enemy within, something the Bible calls "the flesh."

It is a struggle that followers of Jesus will face for as long as we are here on earth. When we leave this realm to be with Him, He will exchange this body, including all the appetites and desires that come with it, for a new, glorified, spiritual body. But right now, on this earth, we live in these bodies, and while we do, there is a battle that is being waged.

Brace for Battle

The Bible describes what frustrated me so much as a young man:

> The sinful nature wants to do evil, which is just the opposite of what the Spirit wants. And the Spirit gives us desires that are the

opposite of what the sinful nature desires. These two forces are constantly fighting each other, so you are not free to carry out your good intentions.

Galatians 5:17 NLT

It took me a while to discover that this problem was not mine alone. This war between flesh and spirit goes on in all of us. It is right there in the Bible, as clear as can be, but many of us make the same mistake I did. We think the coming of the Holy Spirit into our lives is supposed to work like a television show where a dilapidated house is completely renovated in sixty minutes. But God apparently does not think like a television executive. (Imagine that.)

Here is the problem: As revolutionary and exhilarating as the coming of the Holy Spirit into our lives is, if our expectations are different from the way God does things, we can feel condemnation. But the Bible says in Romans, "Therefore, there is now no condemnation for those who are in Christ Jesus, because through Christ Jesus the law of the Spirit who gives life has set you free from the law of sin and death" (Romans 8:1–2).

That is worth memorizing. Let's try it. Read these words slowly, aloud: "Therefore, there is now no condemnation for those who are in Christ Jesus, because through Christ Jesus the law of the Spirit who gives life has set you free from the law of sin and death."

Are you living in condemnation?

You believe that Jesus died for your sins. You have repented and surrendered your life to Him. You have experienced new life through faith in Jesus, being born a second time. You have the Holy Spirit of God living inside you.

And yet, you are living in a place where there is no access to grace and mercy and forgiveness.

You have given in to temptation. You have done things that you know to be wrong, and the enemy of your soul has come and whispered, *You're different from those others. They are real Christians. They are walking with God. They are doing well. They are holy in God's sight, but not you. Angels are singing sweet songs in the night to them; God is visiting them in dreams and visions. They're walking on sunshine, but not you. You're different. You're worse. You're pathetic.*

The enemy of our souls uses all that to drag you down, to isolate, cripple and limit you. You think you are the only one engaged in this battle—this war between flesh and spirit.

Condemnation is a judgment that has no end and no escape. It is not God's plan for you. Condemnation keeps you trapped, unable to move on, unable to become the person you were created and re-created to be. The faith that you needed to receive forgiveness and salvation in Jesus Christ is the same faith that you need today, saying, "Jesus, Your mercies are new every morning, and it's a good thing, because I need mercy every morning. I receive that newness of life from You again today."

Therefore

Long ago, I learned that whenever I see the word *therefore* in the Bible, I should ask what it is "there for." So, when the apostle Paul said, "Therefore, there is now no condemnation for those who are in Christ Jesus," *therefore* means that the reasoning that preceded that word is the basis for the fact that "there is now no condemnation for those who are in Christ Jesus" (Romans 8:1).

You see, when Paul wrote his letters that now comprise almost a third of the New Testament, he did not finish writing chapter 1, turn a page and write "Chapter 2" at the top of the new page. That is not the way you and I would write a letter (or email message). Those chapter and verse numbers were added hundreds of years later to make it easier for people to find what they were looking for in the various books of the Bible. So, when Paul wrote Romans

8, it was a continuation of the thoughts and paragraphs that went before. And what went before is one of my favorite portions of Scripture to describe this battle that we are in—the struggle of flesh versus spirit.

Here is what Paul wrote, including the statement we call Romans 8:1:

> I find this law at work: Although I want to do good, evil is right there with me. For in my inner being I delight in God's law; but I see another law at work in me, waging war against the law of my mind and making me a prisoner of the law of sin at work within me. What a wretched man I am! Who will rescue me from this body that is subject to death? Thanks be to God, who delivers me through Jesus Christ our Lord!
>
> So then, I myself in my mind am a slave to God's law, but in my sinful nature a slave to the law of sin.
>
> Therefore, there is now no condemnation for those who are in Christ Jesus.
>
> Romans 7:21–25; 8:1

Stop and think about Paul for a minute. You may know this, but thirteen books in the New Testament are attributed to him. He planted churches throughout the known world, from Derbe to Corinth. He preached before governors and emperors. He was not the fourth member of the Trinity, but it is safe to say he knew them as well as anyone. That is why I am so encouraged that Paul wrote these words (paraphrased in *The Message*):

> It happens so regularly that it's predictable. The moment I decide to do good, sin is there to trip me up. I truly delight in God's commands, but it's pretty obvious that not all of me joins in that delight. Parts of me covertly rebel, and just when I least expect it, they take charge.
>
> Romans 7:21–23 MESSAGE

Does that sound at all familiar to you? The struggle between the desire to do good and the reality of coming up short?

If you are anything like I am, you have said, "This year I am going to read my Bible every morning. I am!"

No, you're not. You are going to sleep in.

You have said, "I'm going to read my Bible all the way through in a year."

No, you're not. You are going to make it halfway through Exodus, or maybe even into Leviticus.

"No!" you say. "I'm going to memorize a hundred verses this week."

Are you really? What is the good of setting impossible goals? Maybe, instead, memorize one verse this month, with the help of God, and build on that.

Even Paul said, "I do not understand what I do. For what I want to do I do not do, but what I hate I do" (Romans 7:15).

Paraphrasing, Paul was saying, "The things I want to do and know I should do and even have a heart to do—those aren't the things I do. There's a whole other list of things I know I shouldn't do and *those* are the things I find myself doing."

Paul identifies our frustration well. This is not what we signed up for. We want it to be easier than this. So much easier. That is why Paul exclaims, "What a wretched man I am!" (Romans 7:24).

Does this encourage you at all? I mean, not the being wretched part or the frustration of it all. But rather, that Paul—yes, even Paul, who wrote so much of the New Testament and was used by God to start churches all over the world—struggled with this same tension. It encourages me to think, *Wow! I'm in good company!*

And he goes on to ask, "Who will rescue me from this body that is subject to death?" (Romans 7:24). In other words, "I don't like being in this body with all of its appetites and desires and temptations. I hate this struggle between walking in the Spirit and giving in to the flesh."

That is the struggle, is it not?

That is what makes the life of Jesus so miraculous. He was "tempted in every way, just as we are—yet he did not sin" (Hebrews 4:15). He was fully human, with appetites, desires and temptations like everyone else, yet He never sinned. More than that, every time the Spirit directed Jesus, He obeyed.

That is amazing.

Can you imagine going a week, or even a day, where anything the Lord told you to do, whether through Scripture or by your spirit, you just did it? If you are anything like me, He tells you once, and you frown and say, "No, I don't think so."

You drive by a person whose car is broken down by the roadside and the Spirit of God nudges you, saying, *Help him out.*

And your response is, *Oh, look! There's a McDonald's up ahead. I'm hungry.*

Then you are pulling out of the parking lot, and the Spirit nudges you again, and you think, *Let's find out what's on the radio.*

As you drive past, the person needing help meets your gaze. The Spirit nudges you again but you look away. For some reason, however, you cannot stop looking in the rearview mirror.

Then you are at a stoplight, and you cannot forget the person broken down by the side of the road.

Finally, after five nudges, ten nudges, you turn around and go back to help him. A sense of peace and joy follows, and you think, *I should have done it the first time.*

Unlike us, Jesus always obeyed, denying His flesh even to the point of dying on a cross. This is how He can say, "Whoever wants to be my disciple must deny themselves and take up their cross daily and follow me" (Luke 9:23). Considering the many problems and troubles I have had, it would be easier to blame the devil or the world. But the truth is, a lot of my problems, like Paul's, have just been the deeds of the flesh that need to come under control of the Holy Spirit with His help.

It would be great if we just responded to an altar call and God instantaneously rid us of all temptation to obey the desires of the flesh. That would be fantastic, right? But for some reason, that is not how God does it. From day one of my Christianity, I wanted to have . . . oh . . . at least twenty years' worth of spiritual maturity.

Well, guess what? It did not work that way. Instead, it took twenty years (or more) for that day to come. I discovered that we can pray to be more surrendered, to be better listeners, to grow in grace and the knowledge and likeness of Jesus Christ. But we must still brace for the battle. Recognizing that the battle exists is half the battle.

Pleasing God Requires God

When I surrendered to Jesus Christ, I experienced forgiveness and new life by grace through faith. It removed guilt and shame and sin from my life, but it did not instantly make me perfect in resisting temptation and avoiding sin—any more than it did for Paul. That is why he wrote, "What a wretched man I am! Who will rescue me from this body that is subject to death?" (Romans 7:24).

But if we keep reading in Romans 7, we see the answer to his lament: "Thanks be to God, who delivers me through Jesus Christ our Lord!" (verse 25). That is why he can cross the bridge to these words: "There is now no condemnation for those who are in Christ Jesus, because through Christ Jesus the law of the Spirit who gives life has set [us] free from the law of sin and death" (Romans 8:1–2). In other words, we need God to please God.

Billy Graham wrote:

> If we as Christians try to make ourselves better or good or even acceptable to God by some human effort, we will fail. Everything we have and are and do comes through the Holy Spirit. The Holy Spirit has come to dwell in us, and God does His works in us by the Holy Spirit. What we have to do is yield ourselves to the Spirit of God so that He may empower us to put off the old and put on the new.[1]

Paul said, "Walk by the Spirit, and you will not gratify the desires of the flesh. . . . If you are led by the Spirit, you are not under the law" (Galatians 5:16, 18). Having experienced new life in Christ, we too easily make the mistake of following rules—new ones, maybe—in order to overcome temptation. But that is not what Billy Graham and Paul were saying. A new set of rules will not help us to overcome temptation. Instead, we must learn to walk by the Spirit—yielding to Him, listening to Him, being led by Him and letting Him transform us moment by moment and day by day.

Be "Fore" Warned

Take the game of golf . . . please. Take it as far away from me as you can. Someone asked me, "Do you pray when you play golf?" I do. But rather than pray that I will not lose the game, I pray that I will not lose my mind. (Golf is not a game for sane people.)

You may know the rules of golf, but that will not make you a great golfer. You can follow the rules perfectly and never become a champion. The great players know the rules, but they are not great because of the rules. Great players have a gift. They have something inside—a spark of some kind—that other players do not have, and that is what enables them to play at a higher level. That, and a lot of practice.

It is the same for Christianity. We each need a spark, and indeed, we have one. We have a gift. We have the Holy Spirit inside us. He is the key. We were never intended to overcome our flesh and live the Christian life by keeping the law or by following a set of rules. In fact, trying that will only make us miserable. The law shows us where we went wrong, but it is powerless to keep us from doing wrong. That is not its purpose.

We need God in order to please God. We need the Holy Spirit in order to be holy. It is not determination that conquers temptation; it is dependence on Him. It is not gritting our teeth at every turn; it is yielding, moment by moment. It is not an "I can do this" spirit; it is walking by the Spirit. It is not magic; it is miraculous.

In this life, we will always face temptations. But being tempted is not sinning. You need to know that. Everybody is tempted. But the right response to temptation is not to buckle down and try harder. It is coming to God and saying, "Lord, You know my areas of weakness and struggle. Please keep my eyes from seeing wrong things, keep my mouth from saying wrong things and keep my mind from thinking wrong things. Please come and be the help that I need You to be. I submit to Your Holy Spirit and rely on You to show Your strength in my weakness."

What makes it so amazing, when you are led by the Spirit and filled with the Spirit, is that when God answers that prayer and shows up in your weakness, turning back temptation and transforming your desires, it makes you think, *Who is this new creature? The old guy, I'm well acquainted with. But this new man—I like him.*

The Bible says, "It is God who works in you to will and to act in order to fulfill his good purpose" (Philippians 2:13). It is not you who works in you. It is not your willpower. It is not your ability. It is the Holy Spirit who resides in you and works in you. You may not have felt all the work that He has been doing, but from the moment you put your life in His hands, He has been working constantly, changing the direction and desires of your life and heart.

Think about it. At one time in your life—before you came to Christ—sin did not really bother you. Right? You could sin and not worry about it. You could scream at someone in anger and be proud of yourself. You could cheat at golf and be happy when you won. You could put your plastic bottles in with the glass recycling and not give it another thought.

But now you have the Holy Spirit living in you, and He has ruined your ability to feel proud of unrighteous anger or of mixing recycling material, right? Obviously, I am joking about the recycling material, but when you want to scream at someone, you find yourself holding back and thinking, *Uh-oh. This is not a good idea.* You now have a love for righteousness and a heart for other people. You love your brothers and sisters in Christ. You care for people who have never met Him. You have compassion for others, and you realize when you have acted poorly toward them. It matters now.

Face it: You are just no good for sin anymore. You are not made for it. You cannot go there. You cannot live in sin. You have a growing desire for righteousness, a new propensity for worship, an inclination toward prayer—all of which is evidence that the Holy Spirit is at work in you. So, just give up. Give in. God is working in you. He is helping you obey Him. He is doing what He wants to be done in you. Your contribution is submission; His is everything else.

The Way of Escape

Before Christ, the only life we could live was life in the flesh, living according to our appetites and desires; there was no other option. As a result, all we had in our hearts was judgment, guilt and condemnation, and we could not get off that road. But now, because of the Spirit of God, who lives in us, there is another way.

The Bible says, "Where the Spirit of the Lord is, there is freedom" (2 Corinthians 3:17). We do not have to be under the dominion of our flesh anymore. We do not have to continue to be the same as we have always been. We do not have to say, "Well, that's just the way I am," or, "That's just the way we are in my family." We can actually be people who walk according to the Spirit of God. We have His power on the inside of us, helping us.

That is why the Bible says, "God is faithful; he will not let you be tempted beyond what you can bear. But when you are tempted, he will also provide a way out so that you can endure it" (1 Corinthians 10:13).

In every temptation there is a way out. Every time we are tempted, there is an escape hatch, an "eject" button. Do you know what that is? It is basically four things.

1. Set Your Mind on the Things of the Spirit

Paul says that "those who live according to the flesh have their minds set on what the flesh desires" (Romans 8:5). Even if you have the Holy Spirit living in you, you can still live according to the flesh, being driven only by your appetites and acting only according to your worst tendencies.

It is no wonder that so many people in our culture think that we evolved from animals; it is because we act like animals. Have you noticed how body-centric our culture is? Have you noticed how advertising and entertainment center on sensual things? They use sex to sell everything from toothpaste to cars to medicine (*though side effects may include headache, nausea, vomiting, dizziness, disorientation, angry outbursts, more vomiting and your head popping off and rolling down the street*). The strategy is simple: Appeal to people's lower impulses and they will buy it.

Even water bottles say, "Zero calories." Seriously? Water. It is gluten free and dairy free, too. We are that conscious of our bodies and our appetites that we make something out of nothing. We are conscious of and conscientious about our bodies and our appetites to the point of obsession.

Now, let me be clear: It is good to be healthy. It is just not good to have our minds fixated on what the flesh desires, which is why Jesus asked, "Is not life more than food, and the body more than clothes?" (Matthew 6:25). He went on to say, "Seek first [God's] kingdom and his righteousness, and all these things will be given to you as well" (Matthew 6:33).

It is like the proverbial pink elephant. Have you heard of this? Try to stop thinking about a pink elephant. Stop! Put it entirely out of your mind. Forget that he is wearing a propeller hat. Never mind the fact that he is dancing. He is a big propeller-hat-wearing, dancing pink elephant.

Have you stopped thinking about him? Probably not. The elephant will not go away as long as your intention is to avoid thinking about him. (There he is again.) He will stay fixed in your mind. Similarly, as long as your Christian life is focused on resisting temptation and not sinning, temptation and sin will fill your thoughts.

The good news is, there is a better way—a much better way than mere sin management.

When our focus changes—when we focus on the Spirit's presence and leading—we will, by definition, not be sinning. Sure, we are going to miss the mark from time to time. But the Christian life should not be focused on avoiding temptation and sin; it should be focused on the things of the Spirit and going where He leads and joining in what He does. This will bring God glory and make this world a better place.

Have you ever tried to pat your head and rub your tummy in a circle at the same time? I know it is a silly game, but if you have never tried it, go ahead and try it now. It is not impossible to do, but it takes a lot of concentration to do both things at once. Or how about this: Did you know that you cannot sneeze and keep your eyes open at the same time? You can do one or the other, but not both. Similarly, if you set your mind on the things of the Spirit, you will not be focused on sin.

A few weeks ago, a friend of mine texted me, saying that he had been facing significant temptation for hours and was afraid he was going to give in. I saw the text and imagined what he was doing: sitting in his house, thinking, *Don't do it; don't do it; don't do it.* Maybe he was even praying, "God, help me not to do it!"

If so, failure was imminent. Why? Because he was focused on the pink elephant. Temptation never goes away until we think about something else. I texted him back, telling him to leave his house, go to a coffee shop and read his Bible or listen to a podcast I had sent him. When he began to focus on the things of the Spirit, temptation fled.

The Bible says, "Those who let their sinful old selves tell them what to do live under that power of their sinful old selves. But those who let the Holy Spirit tell them what to do are under His power" (Romans 8:5 NLV). You can listen to your sinful, old self, or you can listen to what the Spirit says.

2. Steep Your Mind and Heart in God's Word

We emphasize something at our church called "Project 3:45." The name comes from the fact that it takes people an average of three minutes and 45 seconds to read one chapter in the Bible. The Bible is not only God-breathed (see 2 Timothy 3:16), but it has another distinction: When we read it, the author is present. It was inspired by the Holy Spirit, so when we read the Bible, even for a mere three minutes and 45 seconds, we are tuning our minds and hearts to the voice of the Holy Spirit.

Consider this: When your car radio is tuned to the frequency of your favorite station—say, 93.3 FM—do all the other radio stations in your area stop broadcasting? No, of course not. Those signals still fly through the air, but you do not hear them because you are not tuned in to those wavelengths. Similarly, when you tune your mind and heart to the Holy Spirit's frequency, temptations may still fly in your direction, but you do not receive them because you are not on their wavelengths.

If I had a magic wand, I would use it to induce you to wake up every morning and tune your heart, mind and life to the Holy Spirit's wavelength by reading the Bible, even for three minutes and 45 seconds. This would be before you start your busy day, stare at your cell phone, check social media, get the kids dressed, go to work or coach soccer practice.

It amazes me how so many people long for a word from God that they will drive for miles, pay whatever price, then sit on the edges of their seats in a packed arena, waiting to hear from God while neglecting eight hundred thousand words from Him on the pages of their Bibles.

We never have to lack for a word from God.

You see, the same Spirit who wrote your Bible is living inside you, so He can highlight the parts that you need.

I like when I said this, the Holy Spirit will say. *This is good. Get this.*

Or He might shine a light on a page, saying, *This is what you will need today. You don't know it right now, but you will in a few hours.*

You might argue: "I'm not a great reader. I don't like to read. I have dyslexia. I fall asleep. I get bored."

That is okay. Go online and listen to the Bible. The Church listened to the Word for hundreds of years before people ever had copies of their own to read at home. When you listen to God's Word, you are employing both a modern and ancient way of absorbing it. Whatever way you do it, get the Word in you—not for *information* but for *transformation.* Say, "Holy Spirit, speak to me. Teach me. Tune my heart, mind and life to Your voice."

You know that your spirit is made alive to God when you open your life to Jesus, right? But from that point on, there is a lot of renewing that must happen in your heart and mind. Jesus told His earliest followers, "You are clean because of the word that I have spoken to you" (John 15:3 ESV).

In this world that we live in, filth and dirt accumulate continually in our minds and hearts. But there is something about reading and praying God's Word that scrubs us. Are we brainwashed? No, but our brains are washed on a regular basis as we read His Word.

So, steep your mind and heart and life in God's Word. Take a class online. Get into a study group. Listen to Scripture online. Download a Bible app and set it to send you reminders and notifications; some apps can even read aloud any portion you select. In many ways, it is easier than ever to steep your mind, heart and life in God's Word. We just have to stop letting our old tendencies tell us what to do and, instead, let the Holy Spirit tell us what to do.

3. Turn to God at the First Sign of Trouble

Many of us make a big mistake when temptation comes. We say no. (I bet you are surprised to read that, right? Keep reading.)

When we are tempted to do something that is wrong—I am not talking about a sudden, impulsive stepping over the line into sin, but an awareness that we are being tempted—we often try to stare down the temptation. *I won't give in. I won't. I won't. I won't.*

And before long, we have succumbed to sin. Why? Because our eyes were on the temptation; it was our focus, and our willpower was not strong enough to resist.

The solution is not to face the temptation with a firm *no*, but to run from it—straight into the arms of God. Remember, "God sent the Spirit of his Son into our hearts, the Spirit who calls out, 'Abba, Father'" (Galatians 4:6). So, at the first sign of trouble, cry out, "Help me, God!" The way of escape from temptation is "Lord, help."

To confront the temptation in our own strength is the sure way to defeat. Instead, turning from it with a realistic awareness of our own weakness and inadequacy places us right where God wants us. And then "from his glorious, unlimited resources he will empower you with inner strength through his Spirit" (Ephesians 3:16 NLT).

4. Accept God's Forgiveness All Along the Way

Never be surprised when you are tempted, and never be disillusioned if you fail. It should not be shocking if your Christian journey is similar to what Paul described in Romans 7, where you truly want to worship and love God and serve Him and grow more and more into the person you were created and re-created to be, and yet you find yourself still battling the appetites and desires of the flesh. I know that you think, *I want to be sinless.* But you cannot be Jesus; that job is already taken. But you *can* sin less . . . and less . . . and less.

The question is not, "Will I fall?" The question is, "Will I define myself by my failures or will I define myself by His righteousness?"

When you fail, remember, that is the old you. The enemy will lie to you when you fall. He will say, "Well, see? That's who you are."

But, as Jesus did when tempted in the Judean wilderness, you can respond with the Word of God: "If we are faithless, he remains faithful, for he cannot disown himself" (2 Timothy 2:13). You are His, and He is your "Abba, Father." He is as ready to forgive and restore you at that moment as He ever was. "If we tell Him our sins, He is faithful and we can depend on Him to forgive us of our sins. He will make our lives clean from all sin" (1 John 1:9 NLV).

He will not give up on you, and neither should you.

Summary

In light of all this, "Be on your guard; stand firm in the faith; be courageous; be strong" (1 Corinthians 16:13). As you are led by the Spirit and experience newness of life through His indwelling strength, you will hear more and more the Holy Spirit's words to you:

> Suffering one, storm-tossed, uncomforted, look, I am setting your gemstones in silvery metal and your foundations with sapphires. I will make your towers of rubies, and your gates of beryl, and all your walls of precious jewels. . . . You will be firmly founded in righteousness.
>
> Isaiah 54:11–12, 14 CEB

FOR REFLECTION

- How does it change your mindset to know that temptation is not sin?

- What is one tip in this chapter that you can implement, starting today, regarding your relationship with the Holy Spirit?

NINE

SURVIVING AND THRIVING

THE FIRST BLOW SHOCKS YOU. Your opponent's fist pounds your eye with blinding force, spinning your head all the way around, or so it seems. You reel and try to spin away, but the next punch lands in your gut and you double over in pain. You throw out your arms and clutch your adversary around the waist and hold on until the referee peels your arms away. You back-pedal and lift both of your gloved hands to your face, waiting for your vision to clear. The other fighter wastes no time, however, and you block a blow on the right but leave your left open. Luckily, you duck in time and that punch glances off your cheek, giving you an extra second or two to collect yourself. But your knees start to buckle, so you extend an arm to reclaim your balance. That is when another punch crashes against your jaw like a sledgehammer meeting glass. Your legs collapse. You sway. You land on one knee and hear the referee counting slowly. You drop to all fours, and a moment later your face hits the mat.

There is no more fight left in you.

Have you ever felt like that? You may never have stepped into a boxing ring. You may not have thrown a punch in your life, but I am willing to bet you have taken some. Perhaps not literally, but you know what it feels like to be knocked around by life. Life uses a dizzying array of feints and strokes to keep you off-balance and reeling. It may hit you with health problems—a diagnosis, disease or chronic condition. It might throw mental and emotional challenges at you, causing anguish and distress not only for you but also for those you love. Job stress or unemployment, frayed or broken relationships, unexpected expenses and overdue bills, the betrayal of a friend, the loss of a loved one, a ruined hope or a dashed dream—all of these things can attack, discourage and derail your growth toward becoming the person you were created to be.

Do you feel that way now? As though you are taking a left, then a right, then an uppercut to the jaw? If so, you are not alone. Your situation may be worse than mine, maybe even worse than most, but we all face trials and troubles of many kinds.

It amazes me how many people think that becoming a Christian should mean their troubles are over. That seems almost funny, right? I have to wonder, Have they ever known any Christians? Have they ever heard of Stephen, the first martyr of the Church, who was stoned to death? Or James, the leader of the Jerusalem church, who was beheaded by King Herod? Have they heard of Peter, who was crucified as Jesus was, but requested to hang upside down because he was unworthy to die in the same way as his Lord? Have they heard of Paul, who said:

> [I have] been jailed . . . beaten up more times than I can count, and at death's door time after time. I've been flogged five times with the Jews' thirty-nine lashes, beaten by Roman rods three times, pummeled with rocks once. I've been shipwrecked three times, and immersed in the open sea for a night and a day. In hard traveling year in and year out, I've had to ford rivers, fend off robbers, struggle with friends, struggle with foes. I've been at risk in the city, at risk in the country, endangered by desert sun and sea storm, and betrayed by those I thought were my brothers. I've known drudgery and hard labor, many a long and lonely night without sleep, many

a missed meal, blasted by the cold, naked to the weather. And that's not the half of it.

2 Corinthians 11:23–28 MESSAGE

Jesus never promised—and the Bible never says—that a life of following Him will be trouble-free and easy. In fact, Jesus said plainly, "In this world you will have trouble" (John 16:33). And Paul wrote, "Everyone who wants to live a godly life in Christ Jesus will suffer persecution" (2 Timothy 3:12 NLT).

But that does not mean the Gospel is bad news; it is not. It is good news because living within you is One who not only helps you survive times of trial and adversity, but also helps you learn from them, grow from them and do so in a way that they become an occasion for joy, hope and service to others.

The Trinity Working Together

Matthew's gospel tells the story of the baptism of Jesus by His cousin, John the Baptist:

Jesus went from Galilee to the Jordan River to be baptized by John. But John tried to talk him out of it. "I am the one who needs to be baptized by you," he said, "so why are you coming to me?"

But Jesus said, "It should be done, for we must carry out all that God requires." So John agreed to baptize him.

After his baptism, as Jesus came up out of the water, the heavens were opened and he saw the Spirit of God descending like a dove and settling on him. And a voice from heaven said, "This is my dearly loved Son, who brings me great joy."

Matthew 3:13–17 NLT

What a scene—so instructive, so interesting and illuminating! Whom do we see in that short scene? First, there is Jesus. He is the Son. He is God but He is not the Spirit, and He is not the

109

Father. He is the Son. Then you have the Spirit coming down from heaven like a dove and settling on Jesus. The Holy Spirit is also God, but He is not the Father and not the Son. Finally, you have a voice speaking from heaven, and it is clear that the voice belongs to God the Father. He is God, but He is not the Son and not the Spirit. All three Persons of the Trinity make an appearance in that scene. Each is distinct from the other two, yet the three are one.

I find this scene fascinating and clarifying, because it addresses the "oneness" (often called "Jesus only") theology that you will hear from time to time—the belief that God is not three distinct Persons but rather one God who works in three different modes or manifestations. If anyone comes to you and expresses that point of view, you can go right to this passage and say, "No, you can see all three of them here together."

Jesus is not a ventriloquist or a magician; He is the Son of God in perfect unity with the Father and the Spirit. As a matter of fact, before anything else existed, the Trinity existed in loving, joyful relationship with one another.

The Jesus of the gospels existed long before Creation. We know from John that He existed from the beginning: "In the beginning was the Word, and the Word was with God, and the Word was God" (John 1:1). The Spirit was there, too. The Bible says that at Creation "the Spirit of God was hovering over the waters" (Genesis 1:2). The Trinity was always there together, you see, because love has to have a relationship in order to be love. There must be inter-action. Love must be focused on someone. The Trinity, in perfect unity and diversity, and in the joy and love that is God's nature, said, "This must be shared."

That is why God made us.

Of course, we do not fully comprehend the Trinity. We cannot. I heard one person describe the Trinity as an egg. An egg is made of three parts: a shell, a yolk and the egg white. Each is distinct from the other while also in unity. And yet, the Trinity is a mystery, and any attempt at explanation or illustration will fall short.

Prepared to Persevere

Think about this: Where did Jesus go after His baptism? There was no dressing room for Him to change back into His street clothes after baptism as many of us do today. So where did Jesus go from there?

Immediately following His baptism, the Bible says, "Then Jesus was led by the Spirit into the wilderness to be tempted by the devil" (Matthew 4:1).

What a contrast! One moment, Jesus was coming out of the water, seeing the Holy Spirit descend and hearing the Father say, "This is My dearly loved Son, who brings Me great joy." And then—maybe before His clothes had dried—the Holy Spirit was leading Him into the stark Judean wilderness to endure forty days of physical, mental, emotional and spiritual testing.

Can you imagine? Maybe you can because the Holy Spirit does the same for you. He prepares you to persevere. You might not be aware of it, but that is one reason why many followers of Jesus have learned to expect a deep valley after a mountaintop experience. The mountain is, in many ways, preparation for the valley.

It is not hard at all to imagine how the "family reunion" of Father and Spirit with the just-baptized Son blessed Jesus and prepared Him for the trial that was to come. How much did the assurance and blessing of the Spirit's presence and His Father's benediction buoy Jesus as He strode off into the brown and gray Judean hills? How many times during His wilderness ordeal did Jesus, hungry and alone, close His eyes and remember the coolness of the water, the gentleness of the Spirit alighting on Him and the sweetness of His Father's words?

So it is that the Holy Spirit of God prepares you for what is to come. He sees the storms that are headed your way. He knows the temptations and troubles that lie ahead of you. And He sends whatever will prepare you to persevere when trials come, whether it is an encouraging word, a gentle breeze, a nourishing meal or a good night's sleep.

The Power to Persevere

When Jesus promised the Holy Spirit to His followers, here is what He said: "Then I will ask My Father and He will give you another Helper. He will be with you forever" (John 14:16 NLV). Many Christians are more familiar with the wording of that verse in the King James Version: "I will pray the Father, and he shall give you another Comforter, that he may abide with you for ever" (John 14:16 KJV).

The Greek word for both *helper* and *comforter* in those verses, *parakletos*, is also translated "advocate," "counselor" and "companion." Why are there so many ways of translating what Jesus said? Because the Greek word is a rich one, filled with meaning, and while many individual English words are used by translators to get close to its meaning, none of them fully expresses what *parakletos* means.

Paul used a form of *parakletos* in one of his letters to the church at Corinth:

> Praise be to the God and Father of our Lord Jesus Christ, the Father of compassion and the God of all comfort, who comforts us in all our troubles, so that we can comfort those in any trouble with the comfort we ourselves receive from God. For just as we share abundantly in the sufferings of Christ, so also our comfort abounds through Christ. If we are distressed, it is for your comfort and salvation; if we are comforted, it is for your comfort, which produces in you patient endurance of the same sufferings we suffer. And our hope for you is firm, because we know that just as you share in our sufferings, so also you share in our comfort.
>
> 2 Corinthians 1:3–7

Would you do me a favor? Look back over those verses and count how many times the word *comfort* appears in those four sentences. Go ahead, I will wait.

How many? Nine? That is how many I count, too. Nine times Paul used *paraklesis*, a form of the word *parakletos*. Makes you wonder, right? Was his vocabulary that poor? Was he unaware of how repetitive he would sound? Was he just a bad writer? I do not think so. I think the repetition was intentional. I think he wanted that word—the same word Jesus used to refer to the Holy Spirit—to ring out like a hammer striking an anvil, or a clapper striking a bell.

We lose some of his meaning, however, because *comfort* has a certain connotation. We might think of a comfortable bed or soft chair, for example, of treating someone with tender loving care, or even equate it with the notion of coddling. *Comfort* is a synonym for *coziness, contentment, tranquility* and *repose*. But those restful images are not the precise meaning of *parakletos*. Twentieth-century preacher James Stewart drives home the point:

> [This] does not even remotely resemble what Paul is talking about here. His word is one of the most virile, non-sentimental words in the New Testament. It is *paraklesis*—and that means "calling in to help." It means the summons that brings reinforcements marching to your aid. Our Authorised Version speaks of the Holy Ghost as the "Comforter." It is the same root. It is the cognate word *parakletos*—as in the hymn, "Come, Thou Holy Paraclete"—and it means the heavenly reinforcement summoned to your side. . . . So whenever Scripture speaks of the Holy Spirit as the Paraclete or the Comforter, it is not just the Consoler that is meant. Rather, it is the Reinforcer, the Strengthener, the Giver of power and might and victory.[1]

With the Holy Spirit living in us, we have the power to persevere. I know that often, when we are bearing great burdens and facing tremendous challenges, what we really want is to escape it all.

We want a nice bubble bath and some candles and maybe some bonbons. (What are bonbons, anyway?)

We want less stress. We want easy and smooth. And perhaps God gives you that. Not me. He rarely gives me easy and smooth, but He has a different way with each of us. Often, God's plan is not to give us more ease, but to give us more strength. He wants to empower us with His Holy Spirit in a way that helps us to handle anything we come up against.

People who have zero stress in their lives are either delusional or not doing anything with their lives. (Perhaps they need to grow up. Get out of their pajamas. Move out of their parents' basements. Find jobs. Make a difference.)

As long as we are doing something in life—as long as God has a design and plan for our lives—we will experience pressure and pain. But with the Holy Spirit, we have the power to persevere through it all.

Using Pain for Gain

Why was Jesus led by the Spirit into the Judean desert to be tempted by the devil for forty days and nights? What purpose did that serve? Granted, it had symbolic significance. Jesus' baptism and entrance into the wilderness paralleled the experience of Israel who, after emerging from the Red Sea, spent forty years in the wilderness, where they endured many temptations (though not victoriously, as did Jesus). And there is no reason to believe that the temptations stopped when the forty days were over (see Luke 4:13).

But why did the Holy Spirit lead Him into the wilderness? What did that particular experience accomplish? And what about the fact that after the worst of Jesus' temptations, "the devil left him, and angels came and attended him" (Matthew 4:11). Do you ever wonder what that was all about? Did they congratulate Him? Did they offer Him refreshments? I am being facetious, of course, but

I think it is interesting that the Bible says that the angels did not come and help Him—*however* they helped Him—until after the devil departed. Could they not have come before? Would it not have been nice to have them there all along? After all, angels were His to command (see Matthew 26:53).

Considering all that Jesus had to contend with in the wilderness—the devil, hunger, heat, thirst, dust, exhaustion, wild animals, an unforgiving terrain—I wonder if pain was actually the point, helping to forge the trust, determination and perseverance He would need for all that He would face later.

I also wonder if, after forty days and nights in the desert with the devil, Jesus found it easier to face daily frustrations such as fickle crowds, demanding schedules, troublesome relatives, deadly storms and clueless disciples. Just as it takes resistance to build physical muscles, maybe the pain of temptations, trials and troubles helped build the spiritual endurance that resulted in joy, hope and fruitful service for us.

The early Church leader James seemed to think so. He wrote to the first-century Church:

> Consider it pure joy, my brothers and sisters, whenever you face trials of many kinds, because you know that the testing of your faith produces perseverance. Let perseverance finish its work so that you may be mature and complete, not lacking anything.
>
> James 1:2–4

Seriously, though. Joy from trials? Pure joy? You cannot be serious, James. Except that he is serious, because trials that test our faith produce perseverance.

The Perfect Trainer

The Holy Spirit is like a professional physical trainer or strength coach. Many people pay good money to professional trainers who design exercise programs for them. These trainers coach, cajole and coax their clients through the programs. Why do people hire trainers to do that? Because, as they say, "No pain, no gain."

If struggling was part of the Holy Spirit's curriculum for Jesus, do you think the Spirit can use your pain to produce the perseverance that will make you "mature and complete, not lacking anything" (James 1:4)? Do you want to get there? Well, congratulations! Because every problem you face right now is the raw material the Holy Spirit will use to get you there. He is at work in you. He is using the circumstances outside of you to make changes inside of you. If you are persevering right now, the Spirit is helping you become what you can never be without Him. He is working in you to produce the desire and the ability to please God (see Philippians 2:13).

Yes, the Holy Spirit gives us the power to endure difficulties, but He does something even more wonderful: He uses every problem and every pain to get us closer to the persons we were created to be.

Have you been through a hard time? Perhaps you have lost someone or something. Yet in the middle of that trial, do you find yourself strengthened, buoyed, lifted somehow? Have you been through a horrendous time in your life, and even though the problem is still there, you have joy? Have you been in a situation where you think, *I have no idea how I'm making it but I'm making it; I feel a weird kind of peace?*

That peace and joy are examples of the Holy Spirit at work. His job is to hold you together when everything else is falling apart. He is more alive and active in your life as a believer than you know. I have been following Jesus long enough to have experienced this repeatedly, and still, it often surprises me.

But there is greater benefit to the Holy Spirit's work than merely helping us through our immediate circumstances. Here is how it works.

You walk through a difficult time. It is not fun. The Spirit gives you enough strength to do the right thing and make it through, and you move on. Then, a few years later you are going through a different situation and the Holy Spirit reminds you that the reason you were ready for this next, bigger challenge is that your character was made stronger through the last trial. The Spirit says, *Remember when you went through* that? *That got you ready for* this.

What if, in every temptation and trial, God was saying, *I know you can do this!* It may sound a little crazy at first, but you can actually think of your temptations and trials as a vote of confidence from God.

That is what Paul was saying when he wrote:

> No temptation has overtaken you except what is common to mankind. And God is faithful; he will not let you be tempted beyond what you can bear. But when you are tempted, he will also provide a way out so that you can endure it.
>
> 1 Corinthians 10:13

Did you catch that? He will not let you be tempted beyond what you can bear. That means that whatever you face, He would not let you face it unless He knew you could handle it.

The Holy Spirit is the perfect personal trainer. He knows how many reps you can do, how much weight on the bar you can handle, how far and fast you can run. You are not strong enough today to handle anything and everything, but you are strong enough to handle whatever God allows you to face. He promised that.

That is how Paul could write a letter to a group of Christians and say, "I know that through your prayers and God's provision of the Spirit of Jesus Christ what has happened to me will turn out for my deliverance" (Philippians 1:19). He knew that the point of the process was not the pain but the gain of perseverance that would make him "mature and complete, not lacking anything" (James 1:4).

Of course, we have a part to play in the process. Even the best trainer cannot produce results if the athlete is unwilling and uncooperative.

I have an app on my phone that my personal physical trainer uses to guide my exercise routine. As my coach, he meets with me every few weeks to discern my current physical condition and the best exercises and amount of exercise to help me continually improve. He loads all the information I need into the app. It tells me the exercises to do, has videos of how to do the exercises correctly, and instructs me regarding exactly how much of each exercise to do. It is very helpful. It is on my phone, which means I have everything I need to succeed in the palm of my hand.

There is one thing that the app on my phone cannot do for me, however—exercise. I actually have to show up. I have to do my part. I have to cooperate. When I am in the gym with that app guiding me, it is like my trainer is right there with me. But I have to show up. Showing up is most of the battle. It is encouraging and motivating when exercises that used to be difficult become easier. It means I am improving and getting stronger. Exercise is not always fun. Getting stronger and noticing improvement—that is the fun part! Cooperation with my trainer by simply showing up produces great results!

The Spirit leads and we follow, considering it pure joy and letting perseverance finish its work (see James 1:2–4).

Whatever situation is testing or troubling you, "May the God of hope fill you with all joy and peace as you trust in him, so that you may overflow with hope by the power of the Holy Spirit" (Romans 15:13).

FOR REFLECTION

- The Holy Spirit is the perfect personal trainer. What reassurances does that give you?

TEN

LOOKING GOOD, LIVING BETTER

IT HAPPENED ON SEPTEMBER 13, 2004. For the premiere
of the nineteenth season of her immensely successful television
talk show, Oprah Winfrey announced that someone in the audience
would be given a brand-new Pontiac G6 automobile. Television
studio staff marched out holding platters stacked with small boxes
sporting red ribbons and bows and handed them out to the 276
audience members. Oprah told them to wait to open their boxes,
and that whoever found a key inside was the winner. Then, on the
count of three, she told the audience to open the boxes.

Seconds later, screams of surprise and delight filled the room,
and Oprah began pointing to audience members, saying, "You
get a car! You get a car! You get a car!" Soon it was revealed that
everyone in the audience would receive a car.

It was one of the most memorable television events ever and
quickly became part of the cultural landscape, with Oprah's "You
get a car!" being parodied on television, radio and the internet.

If I may be permitted to make this analogy, the Holy Spirit is
like the Oprah Winfrey of the Trinity. To everyone who experiences

new life through faith in Jesus Christ, the Holy Spirit comes, and He resides within that person. And to every one of them, He says, Oprah-like, "You get a gift! You get a gift! You get a gift!"

Oprah, We Have a Problem

Now let's take this analogy a little further. The audience members received kingly gifts, but that was not the end of the story. They needed to consider title fees, taxes and vehicle maintenance expenses. It is not quite the same, but when we start talking about the gifts that the Holy Spirit gives to those who experience new life through faith in Christ (as we will in this chapter), we find that we must be responsible in the way we use them. This not only honors God, it brings our greatest fulfillment. There are some things I want to mention before we look at specific gifts.

Gifts and Divisions

I have learned a thing or two in more than twenty years of marriage. And one of those things is that it is essential for my wife and me to take the time to have a date night. I admit it is not always easy, but we try to have a date night once a week. We struggle with the same excuses most couples have: "Well, it's really expensive" or "We don't have time for that." Maybe. But it is cheaper and less time-consuming than marriage counseling later, I can tell you that.

We find that there are times when we just need to get away from the kids. After all, how are we going to miss them if we never go away? They will survive if we are not with them for an hour or two. I tell our kids, "I loved your mom long before I loved you, and I am going to love her long after you grow up and move out. If I am really lucky, she's going to be living with me a lot longer than you are, so I have to get along with her, somehow. I told her she could leave me but if she ever does, I am going with her."

But sometimes, a couple's date night can turn into fight night—through no fault of the wife (in case my wife ever reads this far into this book). Sometimes couples might not even get the car out of the garage before tensions erupt. When that happens, they have defeated the purpose of date night. The very thing that was supposed to enhance the relationship now threatens it. The very thing that should help them ends up hurting them.

It is often that way when Christians talk about the spiritual gifts. Paul wrote to the Christians in Corinth, "I want you to know about the gifts of the Holy Spirit" (1 Corinthians 12:1 NLV). The same thing was happening in Corinth that can happen on date nights. The thing that should have enhanced their relationship with God and their love for one another was the very thing tearing them apart.

We see this today. The stitches, so to speak, that should knit us together as a body sometimes rip at the seams as people argue and churches split over what they think and feel about spiritual gifts. Yet God's desire is for harmony among us all, and the reason He gives spiritual gifts to us is to enable us to care for each other (see 1 Corinthians 12:25–26).

A Variety of Gifts

The church in Corinth comprised people just like us. They had the same nature as ours. They worshiped the same Jesus and were filled with the same Holy Spirit. But as my teenage daughter would put it, they were on the "struggle bus." They were riding along through life, struggling with basic things that most of us learn as kids—things like getting along with each other and sharing. As a spiritual father to these people, Paul felt concern for them. He had heard of the things they were doing and wrote a series of letters to encourage and correct them. We know two of these letters from the Bible as 1 Corinthians and 2 Corinthians.[1]

In 1 Corinthians 11, Paul addressed their practices in celebrating the Lord's Supper. They were supposed to be remembering

Christ, but some were focused on feasting and getting drunk. The early arrivers were eating everything, leaving nothing for those who came later. I can imagine they were also giving preferred seating to the wealthy and influential while the poor were seated at the spare table in the garage, so to speak.

Paul approached all these issues with a father's love. He expressed his heart for the people to be unified, to care for one another. And then he explained the gifts of the Spirit to them.

When Paul wrote about the gifts of the Spirit, I think we get a sense of that same father's heart, of his desire that people not get too enamored with the gifts and forget about one another. "One another" is why we have the gifts—to advance God's Kingdom and serve each other for the common good.

Here is what he said:

> Now about the gifts of the Spirit, brothers and sisters, I do not want you to be uninformed. . . . There are different kinds of gifts, but the same Spirit distributes them. There are different kinds of service, but the same Lord. There are different kinds of working, but in all of them and in everyone it is the same God at work.
>
> Now to each one the manifestation of the Spirit is given for the common good. To one there is given through the Spirit a message of wisdom, to another a message of knowledge by means of the same Spirit, to another faith by the same Spirit, to another gifts of healing by that one Spirit, to another miraculous powers, to another prophecy, to another distinguishing between spirits, to another speaking in different kinds of tongues, and to still another the interpretation of tongues. All these are the work of one and the same Spirit, and he distributes them to each one, just as he determines.

1 Corinthians 12:1, 4–11

Walk into any church and you will find a variety of people. Have you noticed that? No matter where you are, the ethnic, cultural and linguistic spectrum of humanity is proof that Gods loves diversity. And one day every tribe, tongue and nation will gather around Him and worship. As John tells us:

> After this I looked, and behold, a great multitude that no one could number, from every nation, from all tribes and peoples and languages, standing before the throne and before the Lamb, clothed in white robes, with palm branches in their hands, and crying out with a loud voice, "Salvation belongs to our God who sits on the throne, and to the Lamb!"
>
> Revelation 7:9–10 ESV

What a thrill that will be! The Church is easily the most diverse organization on the face of the earth. We may struggle at times with diversity, from understanding people who are different from us to accepting customs that vary widely from ours, but God does not struggle. That is clear from the Bible's depiction of the Holy Spirit's gifts and their distribution.

You and I should be thankful for God's creation of all kinds of people. Some of us are great at creating things but make messes along the way; we need people around us who are great at cleaning up and organizing afterward. Some of us are great at solving problems, which is wonderful because others among us are great at creating problems. Some of us are great at assembling things, and others are great at dismantling things.

Not only is there great variety of gifts, but there is also great variety in the manifestation of the Spirit's gifts. That is, the same gift operating in your life will look different operating in another person's life. This is because you reflect Him in a way that is different from everyone else. Yet we all fit together in the Body of Christ for the common good.

I am grateful that God allows me to pastor, because one of the greatest thrills is to see the varieties of giftings in people. Our church hosts an event every year called Summer of Service, or

S.O.S. It involves hundreds of volunteers and high school students worshiping and serving their communities together.

My wife and I were down in the front row of our auditorium one evening during S.O.S., and we watched a roomful of kids singing, jumping and dancing for the love of God—literally for the love of God. We tried our best just to keep up with that noisy, sweaty jubilation, but it wore us out. What a thrill it was to see the gifts in so many people: speakers, musicians, singers, organizers, prayer warriors, technicians and more! It was amazing to watch how the Holy Spirit worked through different people.

We conducted a survey not long ago in our church, and the person in charge of the survey loves to do research. Did you know that there are people who love to do research? Seriously. Not just people who are *able* to do research, but people who *love* research . . . the way some people love football or hot fudge sundaes.

I heard our survey-loving person tell a friend, "Yeah, we have a whole lot of data entry that we need to do for this church-wide survey."

The friend got excited. "Data entry? Did you say data entry? Can I help? I'd love to do data entry."

I was thinking, *Are you for real right now?*

Maybe that does not seem strange to you, but I find it incredible that somebody in the Body of Christ gets super excited about data entry for the glory of God. Praise the Lord! That is far down the list of things I would like to do for the glory of God. It is somewhere below "Spend an hour in an ice-cold swimming pool" and "Clean the dog's teeth."

But "there are different kinds of gifts. . . . in all of them and in everyone it is the same God at work" (1 Corinthians 12:4, 6).

Maybe you have been in a church service when someone is about to sing a solo, and before the music starts, he or she says, "Let this minister to your spirit."

When that happens, my first thought is always, *Uh-oh*.

I have been around long enough to read this as a signal that the singing is not going to minister to my ears. But when the singer starts to sing, if he or she has a gift for ministering in that area, my reaction is, "Oh, my! Wonderful!" The singer might not hit all the notes, but he or she will have something special from the Holy Spirit that practice and training can improve but never replace.

To Each One

In the church I pastored in Houston, we often conducted large outreaches. In one day, for instance, we would feed hot meals to about eighteen thousand people. If you have never cooked meals for such a crowd, believe me when I say that it is a huge endeavor.

To feed that many people, we had a big warehouse, and it had become a huge mess. We had boxes, pallets, coolers and all kinds of outreach materials scattered everywhere. We were also losing control of our inventory because it was all too easy for people to help themselves to the supplies.

So when I saw Cliff in the church lobby, I had an idea. (This happens to me every once in a great while.) Cliff was 65 years old and recently retired, and I knew he was a builder. I also knew that he had been a supply sergeant in the Army many years before.

We really needed a supply sergeant who could bring order to the chaos and stop the criminality rampant in our warehouse. (I was ready to install security cameras and retinal scanners. Or land mines.)

I asked Cliff, "Will you help? Will you serve? If you will, do you know what is going to happen? Our operations will be back on track. More people will get fed. And what is more: Lives will be changed."

He heard me out and then said, "No, thanks. I'm not interested."

I tried not to show it, but I was disappointed. As I walked away, however, I prayed, "Get him, Jesus."

Now, no laughter. That is a legitimate prayer. I continued, "Lord, it's not my church; it's Your church. And I think Your church needs that man to serve in that capacity. More importantly, I think that's just what that man needs. He needs to serve. So get him."

A week later, I was in my office and Cliff walked in. He said, "You remember what we were talking about the other night?"

"Yes, I remember."

"I think I would like to do that."

God got him! The Holy Spirit had already given him a gift, and it was a wonder to behold when Cliff started to use that gift for the common good of the Body of Christ. Cliff cleaned out that warehouse and sorted, organized, filed and cataloged everything. You were not getting a cooler from that man without your name, rank and serial number.

Then he went beyond that. When it came time for the next outreach, he had invented things to make the process easier. He took me over to a table and said, "We can open sixteen of them big green bean cans at this table in two minutes with two volunteers."

How in the world did he do that? He built a machine to do it. When the next outreach started, I came and looked things over. It was better organized than the landing at Normandy. People came up to me all day long, patted me on the back and said, "Good job, Pastor."

And I said, "Thank you."

But it was Cliff. It was his gift being put to use in the Body of Christ for the common good. "To each one the manifestation of the Spirit is given for the common good" (1 Corinthians 12:7). Cliff had a gift for systems and organization, and when he used his gift, it not only worked but it made him happy. It brought him joy. It is a beautiful thing to feel as though you are made to do something that contributes to the common good.

You have a gift. If you have experienced new life in Christ, the Holy Spirit lives within you. That means that you are one of the "each ones" mentioned in the Bible as having received "the manifestation of the Spirit . . . for the common good." No one gets left out of this giveaway. God has given you a gift, something that you are good at, something you love doing. And there is nothing quite like the thrill of sensing the Spirit moving through you to do what you love doing and watching it bless other people and build the Church.

I think many believers underestimate their gifts, or think they have none, for a very simple reason: Using them is too easy and enjoyable. Somewhere, we have come to believe that serving God, rolling up our sleeves and getting to work in the Church is supposed to be hard and painful. But whatever your area of gifting is, that work tends to be easy and enjoyable for you. You may underestimate your gift because of how intuitive it is for you, assuming it is just as easy for everyone, but that is not the case. You are gifted in that area.

I was once accused of doing a bad job intentionally so I would not have to do it anymore. That, however, was not the case: I just was not any good at it. It took me much longer and the result was immeasurably worse than if the person who was gifted in that area had done it. But my coworker accused me of slackness because she underestimated her gift. She thought that since the job was easy for her, it should be easy for me. Obviously, that was not the case.

The Church needs you to use your gift. Otherwise, someone without your gift might try to do the job and end up taking longer, with immeasurably worse results.

Nobody wins in that scenario.

For the Common Good

You have a gift. It was given to you, but it is not for you. (Uh-oh. Get ready for your rugged individualism to be challenged.) We talk a lot about our personal walks, our personal relationships with Jesus, our private prayer lives and our personal Bible studies. That is all fine, but there is a basic problem with that: Christianity is a team sport. In his letter to the church at Corinth, Paul listed some of the gifts of the Holy Spirit. This does not seem to be a comprehensive list because there are other, slightly different lists of gifts in the Bible, which we will get to soon. But let us start here:

> To one there is given through the Spirit a message of wisdom, to another a message of knowledge by means of the same Spirit, to another faith by the same Spirit, to another gifts of healing by that one Spirit, to another miraculous powers, to another prophecy, to another distinguishing between spirits, to another speaking in different kinds of tongues, and to still another the interpretation of tongues. All these are the work of one and the same Spirit, and he distributes them to each one, just as he determines.
>
> 1 Corinthians 12:8–11

That is quite a variety of gifts, and there may be myriad moments when the Spirit will give you a certain one of these gifts. The Bible records, for example, that one afternoon Peter was walking to the Temple in Jerusalem and encountered a lame man who was begging.

Peter stopped and said, "I don't have silver or gold, but what I do have, I give you: In the name of Jesus Christ of Nazareth, get up and walk!" (Acts 3:6 CSB).

Then Peter reached down and picked the guy up, and he not only stood but went running and leaping down the street, praising God.

Now, I know, we read that story and think, *Wow! The disciples walked around with nonstop healing power.* But it is also possible that at that moment, Peter was given the gift of faith for that situation. It does not say he went around town looking for other lame people to pull up to their feet. He did not start "pulling-up-ministry.com." But at that moment, he had what the moment called for. Maybe he had it all along, maybe not.

Paul provided another list of the Spirit's gifts—similar but not identical—in his letter to the Romans:

For just as each of us has one body with many members, and these members do not all have the same function, so in Christ we, though many, form one body, and each member belongs to all the others. We have different gifts, according to the grace given to each of us. If your gift is prophesying, then prophesy in accordance with your faith; if it is serving, then serve; if it is teaching, then teach; if it is to encourage, then give encouragement; if it is giving, then give generously; if it is to lead, do it diligently; if it is to show mercy, do it cheerfully.

Romans 12:4–8

If we were to compile a list that combines 1 Corinthians 12:8–10 (and another partial list Paul provides later in that chapter in verse 28) with Romans 12:6–8, it would include:

- a message of wisdom
- a message of knowledge
- faith
- gifts of healing
- miraculous powers
- prophesying
- distinguishing between spirits
- speaking in different kinds of tongues
- the interpretation of tongues
- healing
- helping
- guiding
- serving
- teaching
- encouraging
- giving
- leading
- mercy

It is important to note that each of Paul's lists is partial; none of his lists mentions every gift. That leaves open the possibility that there are even more gifts of the Spirit he could have mentioned, such as a musical gift or computer savvy. Even data entry! I happen to think so.

I love the simplicity of what Paul says in Romans 12. If you have the gift of prophecy—prophesying is telling the truth of God's Word—then tell the truth of God's Word. If you have the gift of teaching, then teach. If you have the gift of helping, then help. It is pretty simple, but there is a lot of important teaching in those words. He is making several points:

1. *If you have the gift to do something, do it.* Don't wait. Don't deny it. Don't neglect it. Don't hoard it. If you are gifted in music, find a place to use that gift for God's glory. If you have a gift for leading, get started leading. If you can cook for God's glory, then cook. (If you cannot make something edible, please let somebody else do it.) If you love making people feel welcome, join your church's hospitality team.

2. *Get good at using your gift, not someone else's.* If you frown all the time and hate people, please do not join the hospitality team; that is not your gift. But there is a place for you to do something else, probably behind the scenes.

3. *Give it all you have.* Give *generously.* Lead *diligently.* Show mercy *cheerfully.* The Holy Spirit, who gives you the gift, deserves the very best as you use it.

Does the Holy Spirit Play Favorites?

Because I preach in a large church every weekend, people sometimes ask me, "How do you do what you do?" Sometimes they ask it in awed tones, as though I have superpowers. "Super Preacher," that is me. But the truth is, preaching is a gift from God. Exhortation is what I do. It is not always easy; I have to work at it sometimes. But

I am inclined to do it because I consider it fun. In fact, my church currently holds four worship services every weekend, and I am always sad when the fourth service rolls around, because I would preach all day, every day, if I could. I need a nap after preaching four times, but I love using my gift.

When the Spirit works through a person, it is an amazing sight to see, but there is no reason for people to be more awed by my gift than, say, Cliff's gift for organization or someone else's gift for playing the keyboard. My gift is not greater than any other gift; no one else's gift is greater than your gift. In fact, if you are ever in a meeting where a person sets himself or herself apart and above as having some special anointing, run! Why would a person exalt one particular gift except to manipulate you and separate you from your senses, your choices or your money?

The Bible tells the story of a man named Simon who had cultivated an exalted status as a sorcerer in Samaria. He even became a follower of Jesus Christ and was baptized. But when Peter and John came to town, laid hands on the new believers and prayed for them to receive the Holy Spirit, Simon tried to buy that ability.

> When Simon saw that the Spirit was given at the laying on of the apostles' hands, he offered them money and said, "Give me also this ability so that everyone on whom I lay my hands may receive the Holy Spirit."
>
> Peter answered: "May your money perish with you, because you thought you could buy the gift of God with money! You have no part or share in this ministry, because your heart is not right before God. Repent of this wickedness and pray to the Lord in the hope that he may forgive you for having such a thought in your heart. For I see that you are full of bitterness and captive to sin."
>
> Acts 8:18–23

The gifts of the Spirit are not for sale. Further, they are to exalt Jesus, not His followers. The New Testament word *charis* is

131

almost always translated as *grace*, and it is the same word from which we get *gift* (as in "spiritual gifts"). Grace is when God gives us something we do not deserve and cannot earn, such as forgiveness. Or salvation. Or the ability to serve Him and please Him. It is all a result of His grace. The words *grace* and *gift* are virtually interchangeable. So you can say it like this, "God has graced me with the ability to _____," and then fill in the blank. You did not earn it. You did not deserve it. It is His grace.

Those who claim a higher status than others because of their giftedness should not be praised but should be called to repentance. The Holy Spirit who lives in me is the same Holy Spirit who lives in you. When He works through me, there are different gifts and abilities than, say, someone whose gift is playing the guitar. But it is the same Spirit.

You have the Spirit working through you. One of our problems in the Church today is that the people on the stage or on the platform or in the pulpit, those who are speaking or leading worship, are esteemed above the people in the technician's booth or the nursery. That is wrong. That is dangerous. The Spirit is at work through all of us who are serving.

Now, the Bible does say that those "who direct the affairs of the church well are worthy of double honor, especially those whose work is preaching and teaching" (1 Timothy 5:17). But speaking only for myself, I think that those who serve in the nursery and make the coffee are worthy of *triple* honor. Can someone say, "Amen"? My point is that *all* the gifts of the Spirit are worthy of honor and respect. None of us should think too highly of himself and none of us should look at someone else and think, *Well, your gift is better than my gift* (see Romans 12:3). No, that reflects poorly on the Holy Spirit who gave you that gift.

I have known people who say something like, "I don't know. I don't feel very gifted, but if you need help, well, okay."

Never diminish the gift that is within you. The Spirit thought highly enough of you, and He thought highly enough of the gift, to give it to you. It may seem ordinary to you, but that is partly why it is called a *gift* and not a talent or skill. Your talents, skills, practice and effort can add to your effectiveness in using your gift, but just because it does not seem impressive to you does not mean you should denigrate it. You may not see how beautiful it is, but others do. Every gift is important and all of them fit together and make you better while helping the Church to function better.

That is exactly why Paul went on to say this:

> The body [that is, the Church] is not made up of one part but of many.
>
> Now if the foot should say, "Because I am not a hand, I do not belong to the body," it would not for that reason stop being part of the body. And if the ear should say, "Because I am not an eye, I do not belong to the body," it would not for that reason stop being part of the body. If the whole body were an eye, where would the sense of hearing be? If the whole body were an ear, where would the sense of smell be? But in fact God has placed the parts in the body, every one of them, just as he wanted them to be.
>
> 1 Corinthians 12:14–18

If your left leg wanted to go north and your right leg wanted to go south, you would be in trouble. Or think about your foot. What a thankless job your foot has! It is easy to think your head or eyes or mouth is far more valuable, more highly esteemed, than your foot. But have you ever broken a toe? Even your pinkie toe, that tiny guy you never think about? If that guy is not right, you cannot walk right, and if you cannot walk right, you could strain a muscle or throw out your back. Severe injury and disability could result from a chain reaction started way, way down on your little, insignificant pinkie toe. When it is working right, you might never give it a thought. But it matters. It is a part of the body and so are you—whatever your gift, your function, your

133

part to play. So be faithful with what God has given to you. Be thankful with the part that you get to play, and know that every part is equally important.

You Get a Gift

You have a gift from God, whether or not you know what it is. Your job is not to look and compare and say, "Well, I wish I could do that. I wish I could be that. I wish, I want, I hope."

Do not do that. The Bible says that the Spirit "distributes them [the gifts] to each one, just as he determines" (1 Corinthians 12:11). He has decided what He will give you and where you will fit. If you get thankful for, excited about and engaged in His plans for you, you will find satisfaction deeper than you have ever known before.

But what if you really are not sure what your spiritual gift is? Some people are helped by the many programs online that assess spiritual gifts. I am not a fan of them, but if you want to go that route, try them. I have taken some of those tests and when I reach the end, I get a message that says, "Congratulations! You have the spiritual gift of martyrdom."

Just my luck, you know? You cannot practice it. You cannot develop it. You get to use it *once*.

Seriously, though, my advice, rather than taking a test, is to pray and think and jump right in. I am not saying this is in the Bible any more than online evaluations are in the Bible, but I have seen often that people's spiritual gifts are ignited when they look at a role that sounds as though it might be fun, and they give it a try. Jumping in and getting active in your church or community is far better than overanalyzing or taking another class on the topic.

Now, I have had more than my fair share of conversations about the differences between spiritual gifts and natural talents. What is the difference? Here is my potentially freeing (or frustrating) answer: What does it matter? You were uniquely created by God.

You have talents that were deposited in you by God. You have gifts that were given to you by God. It all comes from God.

My son is a pretty smart guy. School comes easily to him and he dominates standardized tests. What did he do to have a mind like that? Not a thing. It was given to him.

Allow me to coach you the way I coach him: What God put inside of you is His gift to you. What you do with it is your gift to Him.

In my case, when I first started following Jesus, I started going to church. Then I saw a need with the youth, and I tried to meet it. I started a junior high class for the three kids of that age.

About three weeks later, I said, "This stinks. I hate it." And I quit.

And I am not kidding when I tell you that I felt the Spirit of God get in my face and say, *If you don't do this in service to Me, there is nothing more.*

I replied, "Well, okay, I guess I'd better do it, then."

I went back to the youth pastor and said, "Verily, verily, not only the junior high will I teach, but the high school also I shall do."

And what do you know! As I started serving—including sweeping floors and driving a van and going to events and just meeting whatever need I saw—my gifts started to show up. As I was faithful in what God had put in front of me, He was faithful in what He put inside me.

A couple of years later, I found out I could speak well to crowds. So they started putting me behind the microphone. Later, they actually hired me.

I thought, *Dear God, do I have to stand in front of people when I do this?*

I felt the Spirit of God tell me, *Listen, they're going to stare at you. Let them stare at Me. Just point them to Me and we'll be fine.*

And we were. I had found my gift just by jumping in.

There is nothing better than the thrill of being connected, fitting in, playing a part and making a difference in the Body of Christ. It is the reward we all experience by using our gifts: singing a solo, baking cookies for the homeless, leading a church administrative board, directing traffic in the church parking lot, playing the drums, planning a curriculum for Sunday school, flowing through the sanctuary after the service and cleaning up what people left behind, pastoring the youth, planting flowers by the front door, typing the church programs, teaching kids with special needs. In using our gifts, we find fulfillment and God gets the glory.

The More Excellent Way

Early in this chapter I mentioned that as beautiful as the gifts of the Spirit are, they are often the source of contention and division in the Church, which is especially odd considering that 1 Corinthians 12 comes before 1 Corinthians 13, which comes before 1 Corinthians 14. That may seem painfully obvious to you. After all, the number 13 usually comes between 12 and 14 (unless you are in a hotel elevator). But I think there is an important point, one that is always overlooked when people talk and write and debate about the Spirit's gifts.

In 1 Corinthians 12, Paul discusses the spiritual gifts. And in 1 Corinthians 14, he goes into greater detail about specific gifts. But there is another chapter between those two. At the end of 1 Corinthians 12, Paul teaches about the spiritual gifts and then he says, "And yet I will show you the most excellent way" (verse 31).

He then goes right into what we know as 1 Corinthians 13. It is often called "The Love Chapter." It is often read at wedding ceremonies. It may hang on the wall in your home in beautiful calligraphy or needlepoint. It is a memorable, quotable, poetic chapter about love. But why there? Why does it come right after 1 Corinthians 12 and before 1 Corinthians 14? Is it like a commercial break: *And now a word from our sponsor?* Is it a departure from Paul's train of thought?

No. Absolutely not. Paul went from 1 Corinthians 12 straight into 1 Corinthians 13 because the people in the Corinthian church had used their spiritual gifts as an excuse to mistreat one another. They were honoring some people and dishonoring others. They were favoring some people and disfavoring others. They were missing the point of the Spirit's gifts—gifts intended to help them care for each other, love one another, work better together.

The Corinthians probably read that part of the letter a little differently than we read it today. We read 1 Corinthians 13 and think, *Oh! That's beautiful*. But the Corinthians might have squirmed in their seats a little as they heard it because Paul was correcting their error and stepping on their toes.

So, after promising to show them a "most excellent way," Paul said, "If I speak in the tongues of men or of angels, but do not have love, I am only a resounding gong or a clanging cymbal" (1 Corinthians 13:1). The point of the Holy Spirit's gifts is love. If you have the most wonderful gifts ever but you are acting in unloving ways, you are not making music—you are just making noise.

Paul continued, and rather than pulling nice platitudes out of thin air, he addressed their wrong attitudes about the spiritual gifts, saying, "Let me describe to you the opposite of what you are. Here's what love is. Love is patient, but you're not being patient with one another, waiting your turn, letting others go first. Love is kind, but you're not being kind to one another. Love doesn't envy someone else's gifts. It doesn't boast about its own gifts; it isn't proud; it doesn't push itself forward the way you're doing."

Paul painted this beautiful picture of love, not for them to sew into a cross-stitch pattern, but to open their eyes about how they were treating each other.

The apostle Peter made the same point:

> Above all, love each other deeply, because love covers over a multitude of sins. Offer hospitality to one another without grumbling.

Each of you should use whatever gift you have received to serve others, as faithful stewards of God's grace in its various forms.

1 Peter 4:8–10

Use your spiritual gifts. Use them to serve others. Use them in love, which will always look like patience, kindness and humility. Never denigrate your gifts or dishonor others' gifts. Use your gifts to glorify God and enrich the Church—always protecting, always trusting, always hoping, always persevering.

FOR REFLECTION

- What are you good at? Could this point toward your gift(s)?

- In what ways are you currently serving with your gifts? If you are not serving with your gifts, what one step can you take this week to move in that direction?

ELEVEN

WALKING ON WATER

I MOVED TO CINCINNATI with my family in 2013. In the years since, I have come to love that great city. It is an amazing sports town. It is a food-loving town with local delicacies like Cincinnati chili, several hometown ice cream specialties, food festivals and more.

Cincinnati is divided roughly by Vine Street, which has been called the "Sauerkraut Curtain." This gives rise to two distinct city personalities: "east side" and "west side." West-siders are known as beer-drinking, blue-collar Catholics, and east-siders are considered wine-sipping, white-collar Protestants. That is putting too fine a point on it, but there is a not-always-friendly rivalry between east and west, a conflict which I, as a recent import, sometimes have fun with when I preach.

Unfortunately, there is a similar division in the Church. It has nothing to do with blue-collar/white-collar or wine/beer. Instead, it relates to the miraculous gifts of the Holy Spirit described in the Bible: miracles, healings, speaking in tongues, etc. Many of my friends believe and teach that those gifts disappeared when the apostles died and the next generation of Church leaders took over. Many other friends believe that the miraculous gifts are just as much for us today as they were for the first Christians, and that we should expect to see them operating in our lives.

Both groups believe the Bible, and both use it to argue their positions. But like the east and west division of Cincinnati, the two sides are engaged in a not-always-friendly rivalry.

It feels like a political issue at times. People have all sorts of opinions and have taken sides before the conversation even starts. But since we cannot get away from the fact of the Holy Spirit's gifts in Scripture, especially in the book of 1 Corinthians, let's look at this controversial topic.

To begin, it is important to notice how Paul framed the discussion of spiritual gifts. He started talking about spiritual gifts in 1 Corinthians 12, and then explained the "more excellent way" of love in 1 Corinthians 13, before getting into specifics of the miraculous gifts in 1 Corinthians 14.

In other words, this is what he emphasized—and remember that Paul was writing under the influence of the Holy Spirit—"Pursue love." As Peter said, "Above all, love each other deeply" (1 Peter 4:8). Love is first, foremost. It is top priority, yet it is often forgotten when people talk about the Holy Spirit's gifts. Love is the goal. Love is the point.

With that in mind, let's look at three of the most controversial gifts Paul mentions specifically in 1 Corinthians 12: the gift of prophecy, the gift of tongues and the gifts of healings and miracles.

Regarding the debate over the question of whether or not the Holy Spirit's gifts are for today, we believe that they are. In fact, we operate in them and train others to do the same. To help those who might be uncertain about the gifts or even feel opposed to this position, as well as to encourage those who want to grow in this area, please allow us to show reasons for our position on the gifts, as well as offer counsel and encouragement for their use.

The Gift of Prophecy

Paul's message in 1 Corinthians 14 is unmistakable: "Pursue love, and earnestly desire the spiritual gifts" (verse 1 ESV). In other words, "Go for it. Just never forget or neglect to pursue love." Then, interestingly, he adds, "Especially that you may prophesy." For people who have been around the Church for a while, that is a surprising turn. He could have said, "Especially that you may speak in tongues" or "Especially that you may be able to heal others." But he did not. He said, "Especially that you may prophesy."

To be fair, some of us hear the word *prophesy* and get a little spooked, especially if we have known many prophesying Christians over the years. There are some who might come up to you—a complete stranger—and say, "The Lord has spoken such-and-such" or "Thus saith the Lord. . . ."

When that happens to me, I tend to respond, "Hmmm. . . . We'll see."

I have known those who approach people they have never met and say, "The Lord just told me that you're going to go to Africa and be a missionary."

I have known young men who said these words to young women they were not even dating: "The Lord told me I'm supposed to marry you."

I have known young women who said the same to men they barely knew.

Now, this is not a great pickup line. And a young believer in Jesus might be deeply confused and feel under some obligation to agree with what sounds like the Word of the Lord. But that is not the kind of prophecy Paul meant when he wrote, "Especially that you may prophesy."

I like *The Message* paraphrase of 1 Corinthians 14:1: "Go after a life of love as if your life depended on it—because it does. Give yourselves to the gifts God gives you. Most of all, try to proclaim his truth." Prophecy in the New Testament is not *foretelling* but *forth-telling.* Old Testament prophecy sometimes involved a fore-telling of what was to come, but in the New Testament, the term relates to forth-telling. That becomes clearer as Paul continues in 1 Corinthians 14:

> Pursue love, and earnestly desire the spiritual gifts, especially that you may prophesy. For one who speaks in a tongue speaks not to men but to God; for no one understands him, but he utters mysteries in the Spirit. On the other hand, the one who prophesies speaks to people for their upbuilding and encouragement and consolation. The one who speaks in a tongue builds up himself, but the one who prophesies builds up the church. Now I want you all to speak in tongues, but even more to prophesy.
>
> 1 Corinthians 14:1–5 ESV

Pursue love and seek the gifts, especially prophecy. What is prophecy in this context? Prophecy is when you edify one another by the Spirit. You encourage, exhort or comfort one another. And we all have that ability by the power of the Holy Spirit. I do not know what you expect to feel when this happens, but my experience is that it feels normal. I think more of us have this going on than we notice. It is likely that this is a part of your experience, but you never realized that it was the Spirit making it possible.

Michael Day was a dear friend of mine who went to be with Jesus a while ago. Long before that, though, I was speaking in Illinois, and I came down from the platform after speaking. He came up to me and said, "I feel that I have a word from the Lord for you, brother."

Now, those words came from a trusted brother, a man of integrity whom I loved deeply. Really, a mentor to me.

So I listened, and he said, "I think the Lord wants to encourage you that you'll never lack to have a good word from the Lord."

That encouraged me greatly because preaching and speaking are what I do for a living. And at that moment, I knew that the

Spirit of God was encouraging, exhorting and comforting me through him.

What is more, his words lined up with Scripture, and so I received them. It has now been twenty years since Michael spoke those words to me, and yet the Spirit of God brings them back often to my mind.

As you read God's Word, listen to Him in prayer and obey whatever He tells you to do, you will have increased sensitivity in your heart and mind. Perhaps, as you spend time with the Lord in the morning, a certain Scripture speaks to you. Later in the day, you might talk to a coworker who is going through some difficulty and suddenly you say, "I just remembered something I was reading this morning. I think this might be for you."

The psalmist sang, "Whoever dwells in the shelter of the Most High will rest in the shadow of the Almighty" (Psalm 91:1). As you spend time with the Lord, He will encourage and lead and guide you in all wisdom and truth. Is that a word from God? Yes. Is that prophecy? Yes. It is not a foretelling, necessarily. Prophecy is encouragement, exhortation and comfort. It is when you go to a funeral and instead of saying something stupid—like "He's one of God's angels now" or "Be glad you had her for as long as you did"—you remember a verse you thought was long forgotten and say, "Maybe in this hard time it would help to remember that verse from the Psalms: 'I will forever remember His kindness to me.'" That is prophesying to one another.

A few years ago, I was engaged in my normal morning routine, which involves coffee, my front porch, my Bible and some prayer. I had the thought that I should buy a particular book for a staff member at our church. I thought, *Wow, that's random. Is this God? Is this me?* I was not sure, but I have learned over the years to take a chance on things that seem harmless if I get it wrong. So, I bought the book.

Now, I did not storm into her office, drop the book on her desk and say, "God wants you to read this book!"

Maybe it is my personality, but the stronger or pushier someone comes at me saying, "God told me," the less receptive I tend to be.

No, my approach was a little softer: "Hey, a few mornings ago I got a sense that God wanted me to buy this book for you. I'm not always right about this stuff, and I'm not sure why this book, but I hope it helps."

She got teary eyed. It made total sense to her. I still do not know why. But when we simply trust that the Holy Spirit is always working and that sometimes He asks us to play a part, we can humbly cooperate.

And it feels normal.

Paul said, "I want you to seek the gifts earnestly. But if you would all prophesy to one another—if you would all encourage one another with psalms, hymns, songs from the Spirit, a few words of encouragement, spurring one another on toward love and good deeds—that would be fantastic" (see Ephesians 5:19; Colossians 3:16; Hebrews 10:24).

The Gift of Tongues

If prophecy is one of the most controversial topics of this debate, the gift of tongues runs a close second. This is probably why Paul contrasted prophecy with speaking in tongues in his letter to the Corinthians.

> For one who speaks in a tongue speaks not to men but to God; for no one understands him, but he utters mysteries in the Spirit. On the other hand, the one who prophesies speaks to people for their upbuilding and encouragement and consolation. The one who speaks in a tongue builds up himself, but the one who prophesies builds up the church. Now I want you all to speak in tongues, but even more to prophesy. The one who prophesies is greater than the one who speaks in tongues, unless someone interprets, so that the church may be built up.
>
> 1 Corinthians 14:2–5 ESV

Paul was clearly correcting a problem in the Corinthian church. They were boasting in their words of wisdom and words of knowledge, comparing and competing with one another. They were not encouraging each other, and the gifts of the Spirit were being misused. So Paul emphasized love and clarified the gift of prophecy, which "speaks to people for their upbuilding and encouragement and consolation." Clearly, he wanted the people to prophesy to each other, and he also wanted them to speak in tongues.

Why tongues?

There are times in life when that which we are experiencing—joy or pain, praise or love—is so great that our human intellect and finite vocabulary cannot adequately express it. How could I describe what Jesus means to me? What He really means in the depth of my soul? How could I possibly express that in English? How would I proclaim the love that I have for Him? It is beyond description. I do not have the vocabulary for it.

So the Holy Spirit has given us the gift of tongues, enabling us to express things that are inexpressible. Jesus described life in the Spirit as "rivers of living water" flowing from our innermost being (John 7:38 NASB)—or, literally, out of our *guts*.

How are we supposed to express something like that? How do we utter things that cannot be uttered? Thoughts and ideas that cannot be pinned down by human language? We need a heavenly language, so the Spirit helps us with the gift of tongues.

Tongues expressed in this manner are for private prayer. They are not spoken for the benefit of others who might be listening but are mysteries spoken to God. A different biblical depiction of this gift, however, shows that sometimes the Holy Spirit gives tongues as a recognizable human language—one that is foreign to the speaker.

This happened at the birth of the Church on the Day of Pentecost, when Jesus' earliest followers "began to speak in other tongues as the Spirit enabled them," and others in the area who had come from other countries to worship at the Temple in Jerusalem were bewildered because each heard "the wonders of God" being spoken in his "own language" (see Acts 2:4, 11, 6).

One of the voices that has helped me on the subject of tongues is that of pastor and author Jack Hayford. In his book *The Beauty of Spiritual Language*, he describes the experience of his sister, Luanne, who received the gift of tongues at a youth camp.

> She had not only met her Savior in a distinct encounter, precipitating a precious overflow of the Holy Spirit that manifested in supernatural utterance, but something else had happened.
> *She had spoken Chinese!* . . .
> She described how, as she prayed, Jesus spoke to her soul—she knew it. And His words were accompanied by a vision that was indelibly stamped upon her mind for life.
> She was seeing Chinese faces—multitudes of them! . . .
> She knew she was receiving a missionary call to China. She would later describe her happy surprise when one of the altar workers told her someone had recognized her speaking in a Chinese tongue. It was a profound confirmation to each person present, for just as the one recognizing the language knew nothing of my sister's vision and call, neither did she know the language she was speaking.[1]

Jesus said, basically, "If you, as bad as you are, know how to give good gifts to your children, how much more will your Father in heaven give good gifts to those who ask Him!" (see Matthew 7:11).

If God gives you a gift, it is a good gift. The gifts of the Spirit are all good gifts. If the Holy Spirit gives a gift, that gift is to enhance your love for Him. It is to enhance your passion for His Kingdom. It is to enhance your love for His Church. Even if you come from a background where you have never heard any teaching about tongues or seen people exercise that gift in healthy, God-glorifying ways, you can trust God. Trust His Word that says He will not give you something bad. He will not give you something that ruins your life. The gift may ruin your love for this sinful world, but it will not ruin you.

Keep that in mind as you follow the rest of what Paul said to the Corinthian church:

> The one who prophesies is greater than the one who speaks in tongues, unless someone interprets, so that the church may be built up.
>
> Now, brothers, if I come to you speaking in tongues, how will I benefit you unless I bring you some revelation or knowledge or prophecy or teaching? If even lifeless instruments, such as the flute or the harp, do not give distinct notes, how will anyone know what is played? And if the bugle gives an indistinct sound, who will get ready for battle? So with yourselves, if with your tongue you utter speech that is not intelligible, how will anyone know what is said? For you will be speaking into the air. There are doubtless many different languages in the world, and none is without meaning, but if I do not know the meaning of the language, I will be a foreigner to the speaker and the speaker a foreigner to me. So with yourselves, since you are eager for manifestations of the Spirit, strive to excel in building up the church.
>
> Therefore, one who speaks in a tongue should pray that he may interpret. For if I pray in a tongue, my spirit prays but my mind is unfruitful. What am I to do? I will pray with my spirit, but I will pray with my mind also; I will sing praise with my spirit, but I will sing with my mind also. Otherwise, if you give thanks with your spirit, how can anyone in the position of an outsider say "Amen" to your thanksgiving when he does not know what you are saying? For you may be giving thanks well enough, but the other person is not being built up. I thank God that I speak in tongues more than all of you. Nevertheless, in church I would rather speak five words with my mind in order to instruct others, than ten thousand words in a tongue.
>
> 1 Corinthians 14:5–19 ESV

These verses make several things clear.

1. Tongues Can Be Abused

The gift of tongues is a good gift, but like all gifts it can be abused. So Paul came right at the Corinthians: "You want competition? Bring it on, pal. I'm praying in tongues more than you all, but in church I would rather speak five words with my mind in order to instruct others than ten thousand words in a tongue."

He was correcting the Corinthian church because they were misusing the gifts—exalting some, denigrating others—and it was tearing the church apart. He pointed out to them that the gifts of the Spirit should produce love, not division.

The Bible says, "God is love" (1 John 4:8), so any gift that comes from God will reflect His loving nature.

2. Tongues Give Expression

The gift of tongues is intrinsically related to prayer, praise and thanksgiving. Remember that on the Day of Pentecost, those who had come to Jerusalem from other countries heard "the wonders of God" being spoken in their own languages (Acts 2:11). Paul wrote to the Corinthians, "I will pray with my spirit," and, "I will sing praise with my spirit," and then referred—almost in the same breath—to giving "thanks" with the Spirit (1 Corinthians 14:15–16 ESV).

Whether it is in private prayer or in an experience like Luanne's (in the Jack Hayford quote above), the gift of tongues is a priceless resource for praying, praising God and giving thanks to Him.

3. Tongues Do Not Take Control of Us

The gift of tongues does not make us weird or disorderly. Paul says, "I will pray with my spirit, but I will pray with my mind also; I will sing praise with my spirit, but I will sing with my mind also" (1 Corinthians 14:15 ESV). In other words, the gift did not use Paul; Paul used the gift. Hayford says this:

Paul firmly states, in effect: "I'm fully submitted to the Holy Spirit in this exercise, but I'm still the one who chooses when and where to speak or sing in my spiritual language—in other tongues. . . . *You* are the ones who determine if and when you speak. Don't blame the Holy Spirit if tasteful order is violated in your meetings!"[2]

When the Spirit of God is moving in you and through you, you still have a choice in that moment. Your relationship with the Person of the Holy Spirit always requires cooperation. You do not lose your capacity to choose whether to sit or stand, sing or pray, when the Spirit is moving. That is not the way God operates. If you see people who appear (or claim) to have no control as the Spirit moves, you should question this because "the spirits of prophets are subject to the control of prophets" (1 Corinthians 14:32).

4. Tongues Build Us Up

The Spirit's gifts are meant to benefit and build up—not tear down—the Church. Paul made the point repeatedly that the attitudes and actions of the Corinthians were harmful rather than beneficial. Paul used the term *building up* seven times in 1 Corinthians 14, as well as the words *encouragement* and *benefit*. He eventually said, "Let *all* things be done for building up" (verse 26 esv; emphasis added). Apparently, that was not happening among the Corinthians; it seems as though they were full of themselves rather than full of the Spirit.

The Spirit's gifts, properly exercised, do not produce division or confusion, but love, encouragement, blessing, praise, thanksgiving and even awe and wonder. To the glory of God.

The Gifts of Healings and Miracles

Jesus told His first followers, "Anyone who believes in me will do the same works I have done, and even greater works" (John 14:12 NLT).

Those words might seem to mock us. After all, Jesus walked on water. He healed the sick. He cast out demons, turned water to wine and even raised the dead.

When was the last time you raised someone from the dead?

Among the spiritual gifts that Paul mentions in Romans and 1 Corinthians are the gifts of healings and miracles, two gifts that, along with the gifts of tongues and prophecy, are often called "sign gifts." That is, they are signs or evidence that Jesus is Lord and the Gospel is true. They are also the spiritual gifts that many of my brothers and sisters in the Church believe ended when the first generation or two of Christians died.

In writing to the early Christians in Rome and Corinth, however, Paul gave no indication that there were different categories of gifts or that some gifts had an expiration date. He listed healings and miracles among the other gifts as though all were available.

Weird, huh?

Because—let's be honest—we see very little walking on water these days. Most of us have not turned water into wine or a snack into a meal for thousands.

So what gives?

Is it because we lack the faith that those first Christians had? Is it because we have access to modern medicine, so we turn to God for healing only as a last resort? Has our exposure to computer-generated special effects diminished the impact that miracles would have on people today? Are miracles more likely to occur in cultures where their evidential effect would be greater? Or, are developments such as mass media and air travel as helpful to the cause of the Gospel as miracles would be? Is the answer some combination of the above?

I think the answer is a resounding "maybe."

The truth of the matter is, healings and miracles still occur today through God's servants. A pastor friend of mine tells the story of Grace, who was so afflicted by multiple sclerosis that her friends would sometimes carry her out to her car after church because she was too weak to walk. That is, until the day she prayed in a large arena filled with Christians and simultaneously received the gifts of tongues and healing from her disease. Both events were instantaneous. Not only that, but Grace and others began to pray fervently for her husband, who had been blind for most of their married life. And though his healing was not instantaneous as was hers—it took a few years and much prayer and was aided by medical treatment—his sight was eventually restored.

One of the blessings of having worked with teenagers for twenty years and working as a pastor my entire adult life is the testimonials I receive from people I knew five, ten, even twenty years earlier. I keep them and treasure them. Here is an email I received recently:

A long time ago, you did a sermon where you talked about being sick one day, so sick that you were not planning on coming to church . . . *but* you read James 5:14–15:

Is anyone among you sick? Let them call the elders of the church to pray over them and anoint them with oil in the name of the Lord. And the prayer offered in faith will make the sick person well; the Lord will raise them up.

I remember you saying that you asked yourself if you *really* believed that, and if you did, then you would go and ask for such prayer and anointing. And you did. For some reason, that sermon stuck in my mind . . . I'm sure it was eight to ten years ago. You may not even remember it!

Well, the Lord pulled that to my memory once again in December of 2017 . . . in the midst of two and a half years of trying to have kids and having no idea why my hormones were not functioning properly. No doctor had the right answer. So I decided it was time to be obedient to James 5. Thankfully, we are at a church that believes in the truth and power of Scripture, and we were prayed for and anointed with oil. It was beautiful and powerful.

Just one month later, I found the reason behind all of my health issues that was keeping me from getting pregnant (funny . . . it all stems from a parasite I contracted while on a missions trip to Costa

Rica 14 years ago). Two months after committing to what I needed to do to heal my body, I was healed! Two months after that, I got pregnant! *God is faithful to His word!* He honors prayers of faith!

The gifts of healings and miracles are still at work in the Church today. I have seen them at work in gatherings large and small as the result of prayer and obedience. I know some people—whether it is the gift of faith or healings or miracles operating in them, God knows—whose prayers for healings and other miracles seem to be answered more often and more powerfully than mine. I also tend to think, however, that the full exercise of these gifts is often impeded by cultural pressures—at least in some cultures—that distract us from prayer and lead us to expect easy solutions and instant gratification.

When Jesus' first followers tried to heal a demon-possessed boy while Jesus and a few others were on a mini retreat up the mountain, they failed. This must have been disheartening because Jesus had already given them authority to cast out demons (see Mark 3:15). They had previously performed healings and miracles in Jesus' name. But when Jesus came down from the mountain, the boy's father explained the predicament and brought the boy to Him. Jesus commanded the demon to come out and never return. And it was done.

Later those same disciples asked Jesus, "Why couldn't we drive out the demon?"

He answered, "This kind can come out only by prayer" (see Mark 9:28–29).

I remember vividly a moment several years ago at a camp for high school students. Every summer the staff took our middle school and high school students to a place called Silver Birch Ranch, each group for a week. For seven straight years, I spent two weeks of my summer in those woods. One night, I was hanging out with one of the camp leaders at the canteen after the students had gone to their cabins for the night. It was time for us to go back to our cabins, too, but for some reason, I felt that we should not go back; there seemed to be something else to do. Just then, one of the youth pastors came running to get me. There was a girl who was claiming that an evil spirit was messing with her.

We went to help her, and I spent some time talking with her. She looked to me to be like any other depressed or troubled teen. There was no demonic presence that I could see. But there was definitely something evil going on with her. She had a sad, dark demeanor. She barely looked at me as we talked. It was hard to get her to share at first. I think she feared that I would not believe her, or worse, that I would think she was crazy. I told her that the Bible speaks plainly about the things she was experiencing and that I believed what she was experiencing was real and not just in her mind.

She shared stories—detailed stories. She described evil spirits that would visit her and tell her lies about who she was, and then she would act out on those lies.

"You're a thief!" And she would get caught shoplifting.

"You're violent." And she would get kicked out of school for fighting.

That was how her life was for a few years. Things were spiraling in a bad direction.

As others worked with her, I kept dismissing myself from time to time to call her parents to let them know what was going on and to verify her stories. As it turned out, she was being oppressed. She knew it. Her parents knew it. But that night she was set free!

I told her that she did not have to live like this. We talked about salvation and what Jesus accomplished for her on the cross. After a while, she agreed that she wanted things to be different. I taught her how to pray about the things oppressing her, and we prayed together. She prayed a simple prayer in her own words from her heart. After praying, she said she felt lighter.

I always find it interesting when people experience a lightness of being because Jesus said, "My yoke is easy and my burden is light" (Matthew 11:30).

Her facial expression seemed a bit happier after our prayer. That night she was given a fresh start and the oppression came to an end.

The most vivid part of my memory was not from that night, however, but from the next year at that same camp. At different times throughout the week I saw her during times of worship, with joy on her face. Often with her was another teen who had been set free from an eating disorder. I am pretty sure I got teary every time I saw those two young women and the changes in them.

Jesus told Nathanael, "Because I said to you, 'I saw you under the fig tree,' do you believe? You will see greater things than these" (John 1:50 ESV).

We may see "greater things" when we turn away from the distraction of our electronic devices and busy schedules and turn our eyes toward Jesus. We may experience healings more often when we learn to labor and persist in prayer. We may witness more miracles when we conquer our expectation of quick and easy fixes.

After following Jesus for three decades now, I have stopped being surprised. I am not surprised when I see or hear of someone being healed, when a spiritually oppressed person finds freedom or when one believer delivers a prophetic word to another that brings encouragement or exhortation. I am also not surprised when that does not happen. Why? Because Jesus told us to expect these things to be a part of our experience, but He did not say to expect them continually, all day, every day.

God knows what He is doing. We are not in control. He is. The Spirit is at work . . . always. But that looks different from situation to situation. There is a fine line between being expectant and being presumptuous. I never presume I know what God will do. I never presume that I am the one who is calling the shots or making it happen. And, I am always grateful and never shocked when one of these "greater things" occurs. If I take Jesus at His word, then I should act as if anything is possible, because, well, with God anything is possible (see Matthew 19:26).

I agree with Francis Chan, who wrote this in his book *Forgotten God*:

> A lot of people want to talk about supernatural things like miracles, healing, or prophecy. But focusing inordinately on these things quickly becomes misguided. God calls us to pursue Him, not what He might do for us or even in our midst. Scripture emphasizes that we should desire fruit, that we should concern ourselves with becoming more like His Son. God wants us to seek to listen to His Spirit and to obey. The point of it all was never the miracles in and of themselves. Those came when they were unexpected, when people were faithful and focused on serving and loving others.
>
> God wants us to trust Him to provide miracles when He sees fit. He doesn't just dole them out mechanically, as if we can put in a quarter, pray the right prayer, and out comes a miracle. Miracles are never an end in themselves; they are always a means to point to and accomplish something greater.[3]

At our church, we offer what we call Foundations Classes. These classes are for people who are new to the faith or have been following Jesus for a while but may not have built a strong foundation. One of these classes is called Basic Beliefs, and we use a book called *Christian Beliefs* by Wayne Grudem as our discussion guide. In answering the question "What is the Church?," Grudem says:

> Not only do spiritual gifts equip the church for the ministry it is called to do, but also they give the world a foretaste of the age to come. When Christ returns, his rule and reign over all the earth will be fully known and experienced, not only in the sinless lives of individuals (1 John 3:2), but also in the glorified bodies of believers (1 Cor. 15:53). As the church, through the power of the Spirit, makes this future promise a present reality (for example, through the conversion of an unbeliever or the healing of sickness), it is giving all who will see a taste of what is to come and fulfilling the mission Christ commanded and empowered it to fulfill.[4]

God still heals today. He still sets people free. He still performs miracles. He still uses His humble, obedient servants to perform "greater things." We can expect it as a normal part of the Christian life. I do not say *normal* to make any predictions about frequency. I say *normal* because you may have sidelined yourself, thinking of yourself as merely "normal" and assigning the "miraculous stuff" to the super-spiritual charismatic ninjas.

Such thinking is wrong. The Holy Spirit uses people just like you. The Spirit's gifts are given at the Spirit's discretion and are always intended to glorify Jesus and build up His Church.

FOR REFLECTION

- If you have always believed that the gifts ended with the early Church, has your perception changed after reading this chapter? If not, why might you still feel hesitant to receive gifts from the Holy Spirit?

- If you believe the gifts are for today, how might you be more open to their operation in your life?

TWELVE

LIVING IN THE RIGHT DIRECTION

PEOPLE FLOCKED TO JESUS. They loved being around Him. He had a certain, as the French say, *Je ne sais quoi*. What He promised others was true of Himself—streams of living water gushed from His innermost being (see John 7:38). This made Him attractive, even magnetic, to all but the most hardened and cynical souls. Such power and beauty flowed from Him that people crowded close to hear Him, to be touched by Him or to touch Him—even to touch the fringe of His garment.

Strange as it may seem, those of us who have experienced new life through faith in Jesus and the indwelling of the Holy Spirit can produce the same outflow of power and beauty as Jesus' life displayed. When the Spirit comes into your life and begins working in you, He transforms you—immediately and progressively—into a new creation, an amazing work of art, making you moment-by-moment more and more like Jesus Himself.

My wife describes the process fairly well. She tells me sometimes, "You're less of a jerk than you used to be."

Of course, "I count not myself to have apprehended" (Philippians 3:13 KJV).

I am not a finished product, by any means. But this one thing I do, forgetting those things which are behind, and reaching forth unto those things which are before, I press toward the mark of being less of a jerk this year than I was last year, and with the help of the Holy Spirit, less of a jerk next year than I am right now. Amen!

But completing me is the Holy Spirit's job. "He who began a good work in [me] will carry it on to completion until the day of Christ Jesus" (Philippians 1:6)—that is, until Jesus returns. In fact, He is doing that right now in you as you read these words. He is carrying on His good work, which began even before you came to faith in Jesus and trusted Him to deliver you from guilt, shame, sin and death.

Filled with the Spirit

Do you remember when you gave your life to Jesus? If you were like me, you thought, *Well, I've arrived. Isn't God lucky, now that He's got me on His team?* Then you woke up on day two and realized that not a whole lot of you had changed. Not enough, at least. Not hardly enough. And you realized, *I need help. I need an ongoing cleansing. I need a daily dose of this stuff, a sort of Holy Spirit vitamin.* Or, in my case, *A Holy Spirit Z-Pack.*

As it turns out, that is close to what the Holy Spirit offers us.

The fancy word for it is "sanctification," and it is the process by which we are becoming more and more like Jesus. The Bible says, "We are children of God, [but] what we *will be* has not yet been made known. But we know that when Christ appears, we shall be like him, for we shall see him as he is" (1 John 3:2, emphasis added). Until then, we are in a process. Sure, it would be great if we could just form a line and have somebody really spiritual lay hands on us and say, "Do you want to be completely sanctified? Well, there you go. Zip! Zap! You're done."

Unfortunately, it does not work like that.

It is a process. Which is why Paul wrote, "What I want to do I do not do, but what I hate I do" (Romans 7:15). He was in the process. You are in the process. You can surrender to that process and become moment-by-moment more and more like Jesus, or you can make a different choice. Did you know that?

You can be someone who is born again, someone who is a child of God and has the Spirit of God living within you, and yet you can relegate the Spirit of God to the smallest part of who you are and never give Him any say in your life. I am confident you do not want to be that way, or you would not be reading this far into the book.

The Bible says, "Do not get drunk with wine, for that is wickedness (corruption, stupidity), but be filled with the [Holy] Spirit and constantly guided by Him" (Ephesians 5:18 AMP). Typically, when we talk about filling something, we picture an empty glass being filled from a faucet or pitcher. We pour the water in until the glass is filled. That is true to the translation of Ephesians 5:18. That is one way to picture the process of being filled, like the song we sang back in the day, "Here's my cup, Lord. Fill it up, Lord." But there is another possibility that I think presents a better understanding of this verse.

Picture a sailboat. (I have a friend who has a sailboat, so I am pretty much an expert.) When you want to make a sailboat go somewhere, you put up the sail and turn it to catch the wind—that is called "trimming the sail." (See, I told you I was an expert.)

The Bible uses two words for wind. The Hebrew word is *ruach*, and the Greek word is *pneuma*. Both words have multiple meanings. They can mean "wind." They can mean "breath." And they can mean "spirit." We find these words used in key passages in the Bible.

When God formed human beings, He *breathed* life into them. And after the resurrection of Jesus from the dead, the Bible says that He met with His followers, "breathed on them and said, 'Receive the Holy Spirit'" (John 20:22). The Bible also teaches that the Word of God is literally "God-breathed" (2 Timothy 3:16).

All of these pictures combine to help us understand what it means to be filled with the Spirit. It is like wind filling a sail. It is the opposite of being "tossed back and forth by the waves, and blown here and there by every wind of teaching and by the cunning and craftiness of people in their deceitful scheming" (Ephesians 4:14). It is the experience of letting the Spirit breathe into our lives, continuously filling our sails and sending us in this direction or that—with Him filling, us following, moment by moment, day by day.

The Doldrums of the Spirit

The Christian life is not a life of perfection; it is a life of direction. What are you moving away from? What are you heading toward? Where are your affections now? What has a say in your life and what has sway in your life? Are you trimming your sail? Are you tacking where the wind blows?

Be filled with the Spirit.

It is easy enough to take down your sail and lose all forward motion. When somebody tells you off and you lose your composure, you let your sail down. In those moments when you lose your temper or lust after something or someone or you shade the truth and you know it, your sail is down. Do not let that happen. Be filled with the Spirit.

If you do let your sail down, however, it does not mean you have lost your salvation. It does not mean you have to give in to guilt and condemnation. You just remember that the Bible says, "If anybody does sin, we have an advocate with the Father—Jesus Christ, the Righteous One" (1 John 2:1).

So you go to the Father in Jesus' name and say, "I'm sorry. Forgive me. I can tell by the lack of peace in my life and the drama that's going on in my life that I need to put the sail back up." Remember, "If we confess our sins, he is faithful and just and will forgive us our sins and purify us from all unrighteousness" (1 John 1:9).

But taking down your sail has consequences. You cannot be filled with the Spirit when you have put down your sail. To use another metaphor, you cannot plant the seeds of sin and expect the fruit of the Spirit to grow from them. That is why Paul made a point of listing what he called the acts of the flesh and the fruit of the Spirit—things you do when your sail is down and things that proceed from being filled with the Spirit. He said,

Walk by the Spirit, and you will not gratify the desires of the flesh. For the flesh desires what is contrary to the Spirit, and the Spirit what is contrary to the flesh. They are in conflict with each other, so that you are not to do whatever you want. But if you are led by the Spirit, you are not under the law.

The acts of the flesh are obvious: sexual immorality, impurity and debauchery; idolatry and witchcraft; hatred, discord, jealousy, fits of rage, selfish ambition, dissensions, factions and envy; drunkenness, orgies, and the like. I warn you, as I did before, that those who live like this will not inherit the kingdom of God.

But the fruit of the Spirit is love, joy, peace, forbearance, kindness, goodness, faithfulness, gentleness and self-control. Against such things there is no law. Those who belong to Christ Jesus have crucified the flesh with its passions and desires. Since we live by the Spirit, let us keep in step with the Spirit.

Galatians 5:16–25

Paul seems to be thinking in broad categories in this passage. He is not reciting a list of every possible sin. Instead, he is reminding his readers of the various kinds of sin that can result when the wind of the Spirit is not directing their boats—sexual sins, religious and superstitious sins, sins of attitude and excesses.

He starts his list with "sexual immorality" (verse 19), maybe because sexual immorality is prevalent and commonplace in his culture. The Greek word he uses is *porneia*, from which our word "pornography" comes. When linked with impurity and debauchery, *porneia* encompasses all kinds of sexual immorality, from premarital and extramarital sex to any perversion of God's sacrament within the holy covenant of marriage.

Paul goes on to mention idolatry and witchcraft (verse 20). The first readers of Paul's words lived in a pluralistic and pagan age much like our modern world. Our idols and incantations may seem less obvious, but they are no less real. We are more likely to be tempted by the idols of materialism, naturalism and individualism (to name a few) than by the worship of the goddess Artemis (see Acts 19), but our idols are dangerous and persistent for that very reason.

Paul's most detailed recitation of acts that result from our spiritual sails dropping involves passions and attitudes that require little explanation: "hatred, discord, jealousy, fits of rage, selfish ambition, dissensions, factions and envy" (verses 20–21). And this is before the age of social media inflaming every issue, before Republicans and Democrats battling for prominence, before people checking their smartphones every minute to discover the latest offense and outrage.

Paul's list concludes with sins of excess, "drunkenness, orgies, and the like" (verse 21), before delivering his sobering conclusion—the reason for the discussion in the first place: "I warn you, as I did before, that those who live like this will not inherit the kingdom of God" (verse 21).

Paul gives us the things that can result from letting down our sails and not being filled with the Spirit, but his final warning says that we could not inherit the Kingdom of God. Do not let that happen. Be filled with the Spirit, and you will not give in to the desires of the flesh.

The Trade Winds of the Spirit

Having issued a clear warning of consequences that can result from dropping the sails of our souls' ships, Paul turns to the results of letting the Spirit fill our sails: "love, joy, peace, forbearance, kindness, goodness, faithfulness, gentleness and self-control" (verses 22–23).

You want to live a life of freedom? Radical freedom? Raise your sail and let the Holy Spirit fill it. As Jesus told Nicodemus in their nighttime conference, "The wind blows wherever it pleases. You hear its sound, but you cannot tell where it comes from or where it is going. So it is with everyone born of the Spirit" (John 3:8).

When you are riding the trade winds of the Holy Spirit, there is no need for a checklist, no adherence to the law for the law's sake. You simply follow the Spirit's lead, and in doing so, fulfill the law's requirements.

If an experienced sailor took me out on a sailboat, he or she would have to issue a bunch of rules. "Put this life vest on. Tie that rope there. Don't swing that boom too fast." And so on. But if the sailor was within me, living inside of me, the rules would be replaced by instinct and experience, and out of that would flow love for the sea, joy in the journey, peace like no other and so on.

So, when you put up that sail and catch the wind of the Spirit, things start to change in you from the inside out. And it all flows from love. In fact, some translations reflect the fact that the word "fruit" in Galatians 5:22 is singular, prompting the suggestion that there should be a colon after the word *love* in Galatians 5:22–23, so that it reads, "The fruit of the Spirit is love: joy, peace, forbearance, kindness, goodness, faithfulness, gentleness and self-control." The fruit of the Spirit is love, and everything that follows in that verse is a description and outflow of that love. As Paul said in 1 Corinthians 13, love is patient, kind, gentle and so on.

Samuel Logan Brengle, whom I quoted earlier in this book, described his experience of the fullness of the Spirit this way:

> As I got out of bed and was reading some of Jesus' words, He gave me such a blessing as I never had dreamed a man could have this side of heaven: a heaven of love came into my heart. I walked out over Boston Common before breakfast weeping for joy and praising God. Oh, how I loved! In that hour I knew Jesus, and I loved Him till it seemed my heart would break with love. I loved the sparrows; I loved the dogs; I loved the horses; I loved the little urchins on the streets; I loved the strangers who hurried past me; I loved the whole world.[1]

The fruit of the Spirit in our lives is love. Love for God. Love for His Word. Love for sparrows, dogs and horses. Love for people, even strangers. Love for the whole world. You may not cry or sing your way through a park as Brengle did. You do not need to worry if you have never found yourself twirling atop the hills in Austria like Julie Andrews in *The Sound of Music.*

Love is not sentimentality or emotion. Love is caring. If I asked you, "What is the opposite of love?," what would you say? I am guessing you would answer, "hate." But consider this: To hate something or someone, you have to think about it or them—they have to enter your mind, even a little bit.

Here is a different perspective. The opposite of love is apathy (and apathy's close relative selfishness). If love is an action—doing what is in the best interests of someone else—then the opposite is to do nothing. That is why God equates love with obedience (see 1 John 4:7–5:5).

When we are filled with the Spirit, love flows out of us and produces lasting joy. That is why Paul contrasted being filled with the Spirit with being drunk with wine; one is a counterfeit joy, and the other is the kind of joy that makes a man weep while walking around Boston Common before breakfast. Most people who get drunk with alcohol know exactly what they are doing. They are seeking a break from life's difficulties. Alcohol does that . . . briefly. It is a counterfeit of true joy that makes you pay some nasty consequences. Rather than remove your difficulties, it often aggravates them. The Spirit of God within you, however, provides authentic joy even as you walk through the difficulties of life.

When we are filled with the Spirit, love flows out of us and produces peace. Paul used the Greek word *eirene* for peace. That word, along with *shalom*—the Hebrew word that formed Paul's concept of peace—conveys far more than the absence of conflict. It refers to inner rest, health, wholeness and harmony. It speaks of the Spirit within that confers peace regardless of external circumstances, allowing us to be grateful even in want, hopeful even in confusion and strong even in weakness.

When we are filled with the Spirit, love flows out of us and produces forbearance (patience). Billy Graham wrote, "Patience is the transcendent radiance of a loving and tender heart that, in its dealings with those around it, looks kindly and graciously upon them. Patience graciously, compassionately, and with understanding judges the faults of others without unjust criticism. Patience also includes perseverance—the ability to bear up under weariness, strain, and persecution when doing the work of the Lord."[2]

When we are filled with the Spirit, love flows out of us and produces kindness: a comforting word in a time of crisis, a compliment, a thank-you note, a smile, a gift, a shoulder to cry on, a listening ear, a door held open, a helping hand to change a flat tire. In fact, the church I lead today, started by my friend Steve Sjogren and several others, grew rapidly and infectiously in its early years, fueled by many small acts of kindness. The following motto is emblazoned on the façade of the church building: "Small things done with great love can change the world."

When we are filled with the Spirit, love flows out of us and produces goodness. Everyone in the world, it seems, strives for greatness these days. But goodness is even better. Goodness extends itself. Goodness stoops willingly. Goodness gives generously. Author W. Phillip Keller wrote:

> It is the good person, the gracious soul, the generous heart who helps the downtrodden. It is they who go out into a weary old world to bind up broken hearts, set the prisoners free, tend the sin-sick strangers, lift up the fallen, bring the oil of joy to those who mourn, spread light and cheer where darkness descends, feed the hungry, and share the good news of God's gracious love to the lost.[3]

When we are filled with the Spirit, love flows out of us and produces faithfulness. The Spirit produces the kind of person James described in his letter: "One who looks intently at the perfect law, the law of liberty, and abides by it, not having become a forgetful hearer but an effectual doer, this [person] will be blessed in what he [or she] does" (James 1:25 NASB). When we are filled with the Spirit, we are faithful to God, to God's Word, to our commitments, to our vows. We may not fulfill everyone's expectations of us, but we keep our promises.

When we are filled with the Spirit, love flows out of us and produces gentleness. Gentleness misunderstood appears as weakness. Gentleness properly understood is strength under control. Picture a bodybuilder cradling his baby. Or a dynamic, powerful speaker holding her tongue (or her tweet!) in a stressful situation. Gentleness is using the correct amount of strength and no more to get the job done. When you strike a nail with one blow and just the right amount of force, it is a perfect sink. But hit that nail too hard and you may end up with a hole in the wall or a bent nail flying back at you. People who lack gentleness put holes in walls. When we are filled with the Spirit, however, we do not snarl or bite when criticized. We do not promote ourselves, but nudge others forward. We possess an internal gauge that determines the correct sensitivity when dealing with people—particularly those who are vulnerable or hurting. We are "quick to listen, slow to speak and slow to become angry" (James 1:19).

When we are filled with the Spirit, love flows out of us and produces self-control. The Spirit reminds us daily of the dreadfully high price extracted by a lack of self-control. Prominent officials, pastors and celebrities ruin their families and their futures by not controlling their tongues, tempers or sex drives. Christians who are filled with the Spirit, however, enjoy increasing mastery of their urges, appetites and passions. Like Paul, they "do not run like someone running aimlessly" or "fight like a boxer beating the air" (1 Corinthians 9:26). No, they exert control over themselves and their bodies so that they will never be disqualified.

Paul said in Romans, "The Spirit of God, who raised Jesus from the dead, lives in you. And just as God raised Christ Jesus from the dead, he will give life to your mortal bodies by this same Spirit living within you. Therefore, dear brothers and sisters, you have no obligation to do what your sinful nature urges you to do" (Romans 8:11–12 NLT).

Is that not great news? This is what Jesus paid for with His body, His blood and His pain. Though we have this battle raging on the inside of us—at any moment we can follow our flesh or we can follow the Spirit—we are under no obligation to follow our impulses and appetites. Instead, by the power of the Spirit of God, we can say, "No." We can say, "Not going to happen." *No* is a wonderful word. Practice it with me. Go ahead. Say it out loud: "NO!" It is powerful and powerfully positive because every "no" to the flesh is a "yes" to the Spirit.

Every morning, we awake to a myriad of options. *Am I going to put my sail up? Am I going to listen to the Spirit? Am I going to obey the Spirit? Or am I going to obey my flesh?*

We look in the mirror. We think, *I am so much older than I used to be. I hate my face. I hate my job. Time for donuts.* That is one direction we can sail. Here is an alternate direction: *This is the day that the Lord has made. I will rejoice and be glad in it. I will hoist my sail and see where the Spirit leads me today. Holy Spirit, take me where you want me to go. Time for donuts.*

We can go into our favorite chair with a cup of hot coffee—you do drink coffee, right? You are a Christian, so you must—and we can open our Bible and pray, *Holy Spirit, I know You're living in me and I know that You inspired these words. I have the Author within me. Will you just talk to me today as I read this chapter?*

And then maybe we get in our cars and start our daily commutes and the real tests come. Some of us are Christians in the garage. We are Christians in the driveway. We are even Christians on our neighborhood streets. But are we Christians in traffic? On the highway? When somebody cuts us off and makes us slam on our brakes? Do you know we have an option at that point? We have no obligation to do what our sinful natures urge us to do. Yes, we can drop our sails . . . or we can turn them to catch the wind of the Spirit. We can pray, *Holy Spirit, I want to put the sail up. I want to be led by You. I don't want to be led by my flesh.* Strange and wonderful things happen when we let the Spirit fill our sails.

One hot summer day, I was driving somewhere with my wife and we pulled up to a stoplight. We stopped, but the car behind us did not, and it hit us pretty hard. As soon as I felt the impact, I cried out, "Jesus!" Not in a cussing way but as a cry from my heart.

Stephanie and I got out of the car. We were okay, just a little shaken up. I went to the car behind us and approached the driver— a young man, maybe 20 or 21 years old. I was not super happy at that moment. I felt my sail coming down.

I said to the driver, "Were you looking at your cell phone?"

Because everybody drives and looks at their cell phone these days. It does not matter that it is illegal in most states. Everybody still does it.

Then I saw his expression. He was scared.

"No," he said. "I was looking out the window."

I did not believe him, but I felt a check in my spirit, as if someone was saying, *Your sail's dropping.*

I paused. I took a breath. I said, "Are you okay?"

He said, "Yeah, I'm all right. Are you guys okay?"

I said yes, shook his hand, told him my name, we exchanged information, and I called the police. I went back to the car—it was idling with the air conditioning on—and waited. You know how it is. When you are stressed, it seems to take forever for the police to come. Meanwhile, your heart is thumping and your car is all banged up and all you can do is wait.

Stephanie did not stay in the car with me, however. She saw the young man sit down on the curb, so she went and sat next to him and started talking, just hanging out. But she left the passenger-side door wide open. The heat was pouring in and I grew irritated. I started thinking "Dad" thoughts. You know, typical things parents (and spouses) say when a door is left open on a summer day. *Were you born in a barn? Are you trying to cool the whole outdoors?*

Then I felt another check in my spirit: *Your sail's dropping.*

So, finally, I got out of the car and joined my wife and the other driver.

Stephanie said to me, "Did you know he was born in such-and-such a place and he has family here?"

I wanted to say, "I don't care. Is he insured? Sure, maybe he needs Jesus, but he needs insurance too."

And again I felt a check in my spirit: *Your sail's dropping.*

The police officer finally showed up after what seemed like three days, filled out a report and was very helpful. We shook hands and started talking.

Stephanie turned to the young man and said, "Thank you."

Okay, I thought. *Now that is going too far. Thank you? Really?*

And again: *Your sail's dropping.*

As the police officer walked back to his cruiser, he turned and cocked his head and looked at my wife and me and this young man as we were sharing pleasantries. Stephanie probably looked as if she was inviting the driver to our house for cupcakes. I saw the expression on the officer's face—a look of amazement, as if he was thinking, *What in the world just happened?*

At that moment, I realized that Stephanie's sail had been up the whole time. The fruit of the Spirit was flowing through her. But I was still reaching for the rope to raise my sail back up where it should have been all along.

This new life in Christ that we have been given is not one of perfection, but it is one of a new direction. Christ has truly set us free. Now make sure that you stay free. Let the Holy Spirit guide your lives and produce this kind of fruit in your lives: love, joy, peace, patience, kindness, goodness, faithfulness, gentleness and self-control. Since we are living by the Spirit, let us follow the Spirit's leading in every part of our lives (see Galatians 5).

FOR REFLECTION

- How does changing the analogy from water filling a cup to wind filling a sail change the way you think about "being filled with the Spirit"?

- Other than the "wind in the sails" analogy, how would you describe the Spirit-filled life?

EPILOGUE

IF YOU HAVE REPENTED of your sins and placed your faith in Jesus Christ as your Savior and Lord, you have the Spirit of God within you. Wherever you go, as a follower of Jesus, you take the Holy Spirit with you. When you go to work, the Holy Spirit goes with you. When you board an airplane, the Holy Spirit boards with you. When you walk into a shop, the Holy Spirit enters with you. Whatever you do, wherever you go, the Holy Spirit is with you and within you.

He is within, to affirm that you are God's child (see Romans 8:16).

He is within, to convict you of sin and turn you back to the Father (see 1 Thessalonians 1:5).

He is within, to teach you and remind you of everything God wants you to know (see John 14:26).

He is within, to pray for you, with you and in you—and you in Him (see Romans 8:26–27).

He is within, to help you resist temptation and grow more and more into the person God created you to be (see Galatians 5:16).

He is within, to enable you not only to persevere through hard times, but to emerge stronger and better (see Romans 15:13, Philippians 1:19).

He is within, to empower you with gifts that will help you serve others and build up the Church (see 1 Corinthians 12–14, Romans 12:3–8).

He is within, to produce fruit in keeping with repentance (see Matthew 3:8, Luke 3:8).

He is within, to fill you and sail your life in the right direction (see Ephesians 5:18).

Finally, He is within, to make you courageous and ready to tell others what God in Christ has done for you. What Paul said about the early Church in Corinth is true also of you: "You are a letter from Christ . . . written not with ink but with the Spirit of the living God, not on tablets of stone but on tablets of human hearts. Such confidence we have through Christ before God" (2 Corinthians 3:3–4).

Before the Holy Spirit was given, Jesus' first followers were what we might call today "a mess." They often exasperated Jesus and embarrassed themselves. At the moment when their support was most needed and courage most called for—when Jesus faced arrest, trial and execution—they panicked and fled.

But after they received the Holy Spirit, it was their fear that fled. R. T. Kendall wrote, "Total fearlessness is what Peter had on the Day of Pentecost. No fear. He was not the slightest bit bothered by thousands of intimidating Jews around him—some of them high ranking."[1]

What does total fearlessness feel like? It is not ignorance or naïveté. Peter knew exactly what was going on and what the stakes were. The Holy Spirit enabled him to have enough courage to do and say exactly what God wanted him to do and say. That can be true of us as well, regardless of whether or not we think "total fearlessness" is even attainable. The point is that Peter was a much different man because he was fearing less and less.

Sometime after Pentecost, John and Peter were heading to the Temple in Jerusalem to pray. As they were about to enter the gate everyone called "Beautiful," they encountered a man who was always there begging. The beggar asked for a donation. But though they may have passed that man hundreds of times before—and may have given him money on multiple occasions—this time they responded differently.

Peter said, "Silver or gold I do not have, but what I do have I give you. In the name of Jesus Christ of Nazareth, walk" (Acts 3:6).

And they helped him to his feet. "Instantly the man's feet and ankles became strong. He jumped to his feet and began to walk. Then he went with them into the temple courts, walking and jumping, and praising God" (Acts 3:7–8). Of course, people gathered around, looking with amazement at the former lame beggar walking with John and Peter, wondering, *Who are these people?*

Well, Peter was the one who denied Jesus, who failed Him when the chips were down. But now he had the Holy Spirit within. He seized the opportunity and addressed the crowd that gathered, saying:

> "Fellow Israelites, why does this surprise you? Why do you stare at us as if by our own power or godliness we had made this man walk? . . . By faith in the name of Jesus, this man whom you see and know was made strong. It is Jesus' name and the faith that comes through him that has completely healed him, as you can all see."
>
> Acts 3:12, 16

Peter—the same guy who ran and hid just weeks earlier—made this bold declaration in front of everyone because of the Holy Spirit who was within him.

Of course, this did not make the religious leaders in Jerusalem happy. "They were greatly disturbed because the apostles were teaching the people, proclaiming in Jesus the resurrection of the dead" (Acts 4:2).

Have you ever had a conversation with somebody—talking about, say, sports, weather, movies, maybe even politics—and then something changes when you mention the name of Jesus?

There is something about that name that causes people to get defensive, even offended. That is what Peter and John experienced. The authorities hauled them off to jail, where they spent the night. The next day, "They had Peter and John brought before them and began to question them: 'By what power or what name did you do this?'" (Acts 4:7).

Then the guy who had denied Jesus in front of a servant girl (and later, two other people) before His crucifixion, stood up—facing imprisonment, even death—and being filled with the Holy Spirit, said:

> "Rulers and elders of the people! If we are being called to account today for an act of kindness shown to a man who was lame and are being asked how he was healed, then know this, you and all the people of Israel: It is by the name of Jesus Christ of Nazareth, whom you crucified but whom God raised from the dead, that this man stands before you healed. Jesus is 'the stone you builders rejected, which has become the cornerstone.' Salvation is found in no one else, for there is no other name under heaven given to mankind by which we must be saved."
>
> Acts 4:8–12

Then he dropped the microphone.

The difference in Peter's behavior—the secret of his transformation from a denying disciple to a man on a mission—was the Holy Spirit within. The authorities even asked, "You're upsetting everybody. Would you please just kind of . . . Could you just stop?"

Peter and John answered, "We cannot."

The account goes on to say that they went from there to a prayer meeting and prayed, "God, would you give us more boldness?" After all that? More boldness? And guess what happened then? The Bible says, "After they prayed, the place where they were meeting was shaken. And they were all filled with the Holy Spirit and spoke the word of God boldly" (Acts 4:31). Their sails were up, the Holy Spirit filled them and they spoke about Jesus with even greater boldness.

The Holy Spirit is within you to make you fearless and bold in telling others what God in Christ has done for you, to make you unashamed of Jesus, unashamed of the Gospel "because it is the power of God that brings salvation to everyone who believes" (Romans 1:16).

Come on, admit it. Many of us are somewhere between awkward and afraid when it comes to talking with others about Jesus. Doesn't that seem a bit crazy? It makes little sense that we would be hesitant to share with others the best thing that has ever happened to us. Yet for some reason, we often are, which I submit as "Exhibit A" for my contention that there is a spiritual battle going on. Satan fights against the purposes of God because he wants to steal the glory of God. He wants people to remain spiritually blind.

> Satan, who is the god of this world, has blinded the minds of those who don't believe. They are unable to see the glorious light of the Good News. They don't understand this message about the glory of Christ, who is the exact likeness of God.
>
> You see, we don't go around preaching about ourselves. We preach that Jesus Christ is Lord, and we ourselves are your servants for Jesus' sake. For God, who said, "Let there be light in the darkness," has made this light shine in our hearts so we could know the glory of God that is seen in the face of Jesus Christ.
>
> 2 Corinthians 4:4–6 NLT

I have good news for you. Sharing Jesus with others is also a work of the Spirit. It is not all on you, just as it was not all on Peter. My former pastor at Christ Community Church in St. Charles, Illinois, teaches that we should pray for *open doors*—opportunities that the Spirit orchestrates; *open hearts*—the work of the Spirit to make someone receptive to His truth; and *open mouths*—when the Spirit makes us aware of the opportunity and helps us to say helpful things. Most of us do not think of ourselves as evangelists, but when we simply cooperate with what the Spirit is doing, our lives end up helping many other people meet Jesus.

The Holy Spirit is within you. Be conscious of Him. Cooperate with Him. Be filled with Him. Be bold in Him. And ride the winds of the Spirit wherever and to whomever He sends you.

APPENDIX

DURING THE WRITING OF THIS BOOK, many good questions were asked that did not fit well into any chapter. Good questions deserve good answers, so here are some that you might find helpful.

I don't want to be weird or perceived of as weird, but sometimes I feel led by the Holy Spirit to do something that might seem weird. Should I be concerned by this?

Good question! I am glad you want to be what we call "naturally supernatural." There is no doubt that the Holy Spirit will guide us to attempt to accomplish things we would never be able to accomplish on our own. He knows exactly what needs to be done, and sometimes those things might seem odd or out of the ordinary to us. In such cases, how you go about them is more important than anything else.

If you are humble and communicate things in a way that somebody else can receive them, that is most of the battle. Imagine, for example, that you are at an event and sense the Holy Spirit directing you to go and pray for someone. Instead of walking up to the person and saying, "Hey, God just told me to come over and pray for you," you might say, "Excuse me, would it be okay if I pray for you?"

The person might ask why. Then you could gently say that you felt the Lord was asking you to do so. Chances are, the people you approach in this way will be appreciative and receptive because the Holy Spirit knows what they need, when they need it.

We do not need to come across as super-spiritual ninjas; that is normally what others react negatively to. If we are intentionally humble and gentle in our approach, people will receive us as normal people who are part of the normal Christian life.

Let all things be done naturally. Naturally supernatural.

Your book seems to talk about the role of the Holy Spirit in our everyday lives. What about during worship services?

The answer to this question depends somewhat on the size of the congregation. Allow me to explain.

We are instructed not to quench the Spirit and to desire the Holy Spirit's gifts. The apostle Paul seems to go out of his way to coach the Corinthian church in how to do both in their gatherings while also taking into consideration practical issues such as the presence of nonbelievers or new Christians. There is no doubt that we do not want to quench the Spirit—the gifts strengthen the Church. But there are practical considerations for a gathering: Things should be edifying, helpful and in order.

Let me give an illustration. The room in which we meet for our weekend services has more than two thousand seats. That means a lot of people. Can you imagine someone standing up during the worship service, interrupting what is going on and saying he or she has a prophetic word for the people? That raises all kinds of issues. In the first place a word like that could be confusing in a room that big since not everyone would be able to hear. Further questions come to mind: Does anyone know this person? Is this a credible, mature believer? So many things to consider.

The gifts of the Spirit are wonderful and best expressed in the context of relationally connected believers—gatherings where people know each other. As a church grows, at a certain point, that will no longer be true of its weekend worship services. But it will likely be true of small-group Bible studies, prayer meetings, serving teams, retreats or simply being in relationship with one another. And when the gifts are expressed in any of those gatherings, all things must be done decently and in order.

So, yes, do not quench the Spirit. And, yes, desire the gifts. And, yes, use your mind to consider practical things and enjoy the freedom you have in Jesus to figure these kinds of things out in the life of your church. Remember that having the Holy Spirit within you is always a matter of cooperation.

Things can be Spirit-led and also organized and orderly. Church meetings should not be confusing or out of control.

How did you personally discover what your spiritual gifts are?

One word: *serving.* Okay, now for more than one word.

The Spirit of God accomplishes the mission of God. God's purposes are moving forward in human history, and we are equipped by the Spirit to play a part in that. When we are participating in what God is doing, that is when we start to recognize how the Holy Spirit is enabling us to be effective. That is serving—playing our part.

My advice, then, is to go ahead and jump in and always stay engaged in serving in some capacity in the life of your church. As you do, you will start to learn that there are certain things that not only come easier to you, but are enjoyable as well!

When it comes to your areas of giftedness, it is likely that you discount being gifted in the areas that come easily to you. You naturally think that because it is an easy thing for you, it is common and easy for everyone—nothing special.

In all likelihood, it is not common. You might be surprised when others tell you how good you are at something that they either dislike or cannot do with any competence. Let that be your clue to discovering how you have been gifted by the Holy Spirit.

I have also learned that discovering your giftings often requires stepping out of your comfort zone. When faced with new challenges and new responsibilities, you often have the joy of seeing what the Spirit wants to do in you and through you to accomplish His purposes.

If this answer seems a bit rambling, just remember this: Serve first; discover second. Trying to discover before serving is like trying to figure out what position will be best for you on a team without ever playing the sport.

Lace up your cleats and join the team.

I'm a leader in my church, and I don't agree with our stated beliefs regarding the Holy Spirit. What do I do?

Wow! That can be a tricky one, especially if you receive your paycheck from the church.

I have been in that situation a few times. First, I would say to take the opportunity to investigate why you believe what you believe. That will be important for the rest of your life. Study the Scriptures. Then you have to ask yourself if it is such a huge disagreement that your integrity is at stake. Chances are, that is not likely the case unless your church has an extreme view on certain things.

Christians can always do better at having gracious conversations. Perhaps you could ask the church leaders to discuss with you how they view things so that you can better appreciate their positions.

In terms of teaching, my approach has always been to teach the core of a topic and then help people navigate the various views that Christians might hold. It is very important to teach your church's view if you agreed to do so. If you are on staff, you agreed implicitly to do so unless some other agreement has been made explicitly. You can teach the view of the church without saying it is your personal view. I have said things such as, "I have my own thoughts on the matter, but the goal of this class is not to teach you what I think, but rather the biblically based practices of our church."

If you cannot do that humbly and in a spirit of unity, then it is better to be quiet. You never want to cause division or stir up dissension. Always make sure that whatever you do, you are on the same page with your pastor(s). In any case, the particular view of your church does not negate your ability to live the kind of life we are championing in this book.

Can a person have multiple gifts, or are there primary and secondary gifts?

The Bible tells us that the Holy Spirit distributes the gifts. We are not told much more than that with any specificity. Chances are that you will begin to notice that you have a few gifts that are in play most of the time. It is also very possible that from time to time, the Holy Spirit will give you the ability to do something that is not your norm. Let me add here that the words *gift* and *grace* are pretty much the same word. That helps me remember that God gives me something that I do not deserve or earn. He is the one doing that. So, whether you consider your gifts primary or secondary, or permanent or temporary, it is all from Him.

My coaching here is to tell you always to remain open to the extravagant grace and love of God. That means we remain open to His doing wonderful things in us and through us. Many Christians suffer from the "paralysis of analysis."

Don't overthink a gift. Just open it.

Do you have to have a gift of the Spirit to be a Christian?

Oh, I bet I know where this question is coming from. This can get confusing, so bear with me.

Pentecostal churches teach that speaking in tongues is *the* evidence of being filled with the Spirit (or what is also referred to as being baptized with the Spirit). Then that logic is taken one step further. It goes something like this: If you have repented and put your faith in Jesus, then the Spirit of God lives within you. If you have the Spirit, you will speak in tongues. Therefore, if you do not speak in tongues, you are not a true believer (i.e.—not saved).

What is helpful to know is that this is not a commonly held view. Also, the evidence of a Spirit-filled life is the fruit of the Spirit: love, joy, peace, patience, kindness, goodness, gentleness, perseverance and self-control.

Tongues is a wonderful gift. It is not the proof that you are, in fact, a Christian.

Why do some people talk about a "second work" of the Spirit after salvation?

Another whopper of a question! Handling this question well goes way beyond a one-paragraph answer. But, hey, let's give it a shot anyway.

When you place your faith in Jesus, the Holy Spirit takes up residence within you. Scripture (especially Acts) also describes what seems to be a second thing called being "baptized with the Spirit." We are further coached in the Bible to be filled with the Spirit again and again (see Ephesians 5:18–20).

There are many great books out there on this topic. You should read them. Keep learning and growing. The goal of this book is to help us all cooperate with the Helper who lives within us. Yes, this book is biblically solid. But is it the world's greatest theological treatise on the nuances of how the Spirit of God is talked about in the New Testament? No.

For the purposes of this book, I would say that we should not think in terms of first and second works of the Holy Spirit, but rather of ongoing cooperation with the Helper from the first day we placed our faith in Jesus.

Flow continually with the ongoing work of the Spirit. If you do that, you will not have to worry about missing out on any "second" work. He will help you because . . . well . . . He is the Helper.

Why do some people have the gift of healing? Can't we all pray for others to be healed?

I don't know. Yes. Moving on. (Just kidding.)

The truth is, we do not know why or how the Spirit chooses to distribute the gifts. God knows what He is doing.

I think things get a little weird for us when we think about healing because we have seen too many charlatan faith healers and other abuses when it comes to this particular gift.

I would like to remind you to build your faith on the bedrock of the Bible, not as a reaction to the excesses, abuses or just plain weirdness of others. Physical healing does happen, and some people are gifted to see this happen with more regularity. Certainly, pray for people to receive healing even if you do not consider yourself as a person who has the gift of healing. There is no pressure on you. It is God who heals, not us.

Here is an analogy: Have you ever met people with the gift of evangelism? They seem to slide easily into conversations with folks about Jesus, bringing lots of people to church and seeing what seems to be more than their fair share of people coming to faith. That is the gift of evangelism. Yet this in no way means that the rest of us are off the hook when it comes to sharing the Good News with others or just being good inviters.

Remember that whatever desire and effectiveness you are experiencing, accomplishing the purposes of God comes from the Helper.

Should we pray to the Holy Spirit?

I am guessing that you have prayed to Jesus. Maybe a lot. And to the Father? Likely. And I hope that after reading this book, you find yourself asking the Holy Spirit for some help and direction. Since the Trinity is in perfect unity, I am pretty sure they can handle the processing of your prayers. Remember that whole "package deal" stuff we talked about in this book? The Bible gives us descriptions of each of the three Persons of the Trinity being addressed in prayer.

Your prayers will not get lost in the mail.

Why do you think there is so much disagreement or fear about the Holy Spirit?

Think about a car without gas. A lamp without electricity. They cannot accomplish the purposes for which they were created. They look like a car and a lamp. They just do not function like a car and a lamp.

I think Satan knows that the Church cannot be effective without the Helper. Jesus thought the same thing. Remember, Jesus is the One who told us not even to try to minister without the Helper. So, if I am trying to thwart the purposes of God, I am going to do everything I can to stir up confusion, fear, disagreement and dismissal regarding the Holy Spirit. It is a spiritual tactic of the enemy. Do you want to keep a car from running? Siphon out the gas. Do you want to keep a lamp from working? Unplug it. Do you want to keep the Church from being effective? Ignore the Helper.

Have you read the end of the book? No, not this one—the Bible. One day the struggle is over. God wins. And everything is made perfect again. But we do not live there yet. We still live in the struggle. And the enemy of God would like nothing more than for us to spend our time arguing about the Holy Spirit instead of cooperating with the Holy Spirit.

NOTES

Chapter 1: The Quest for More

1. Henry David Thoreau, *Walden* (Garden City, N.J.: International Collectors Library, 1970), 7.

Chapter 4: The Promise and the Package

1. Billy Graham, *The Holy Spirit: Activating God's Power in Your Life* (Waco: Word Books, 1978), 30.

Chapter 5: Living Confidently

1. Portions of this chapter are drawn from a message Raul Latoni delivered at Vineyard Cincinnati in July 2017.
2. John Wesley, *Sermons on Several Occasions* (Hudson: William E. Norman, 1810), 311.
3. Fanny Crosby, "Blessed Assurance," public domain.
4. Phillips Brooks, "O Little Town of Bethlehem," public domain.

Chapter 6: Living with Clarity

1. R. A. Torrey, *The Holy Spirit: Who He Is and What He Does* (Old Tappan, N.J.; Revell, 1927), 43, emphasis added.
2. Charles G. Finney, *An Autobiography* (Old Tappan, N.J.: Revell, 1908), 183–84.
3. J. I. Packer, *Keep In Step With the Spirit* (Old Tappan, N.J.: Revell, 1984), 66.

Chapter 7: Living in Good Company

1. Andrew Murray, *With Christ in the School of Prayer* (New Kensington, Penn.: Whitaker House, 1981), 189.

2. We will talk more about the gifts of the Spirit in chapter 11.

3. Samuel Logan Brengle, *Come Holy Guest* (Indianapolis: Wesleyan Publishing House, 2016), 227.

4. A. W. Tozer, *This World: Playground or Battleground?* (Camp Hill, Penn.: Christian Publications, 1989), 16.

Chapter 8: Growing More Like the Person God Created You to Be

1. Billy Graham, *The Holy Spirit: Activating God's Power in Your Life* (Waco: Word Books, 1978), 88.

Chapter 9: Surviving and Thriving

1. James S. Stewart, *The Wind of the Spirit* (Nashville: Abingdon Press, 1968), 149.

Chapter 10: Looking Good, Living Better

1. First Corinthians 5:9 reveals that there were at least three, the first of which has apparently been lost to us.

Chapter 11: Walking on Water

1. Jack Hayford, *The Beauty of Spiritual Language: Unveiling the Mystery of Speaking in Tongues* (Southlake, Tex.: Gateway Press, 2018), 35–37.

2. Hayford, 48.

3. Francis Chan, *Forgotten God* (Colorado Springs: David C. Cook, 2009), 88.

4. Wayne A. Grudem, *Christian Beliefs: Twenty Basics Every Christian Should Know* (Grand Rapids, Mich.: Zondervan, 2005), 118.

Chapter 12: Living in the Right Direction

1. Samuel Logan Brengle, *Helps to Holiness* (Indianapolis: Wesleyan Publishing House, 2016), 9–10.

2. Billy Graham, *The Holy Spirit: Activating God's Power in Your Life* (Waco: Word Books, 1978), 195–196.

3. W. Phillip Keller, *A Gardener Looks at the Fruits of the Spirit* (Waco: Word Books, 1979), 146.

Epilogue

1. R. T. Kendall, *Holy Fire: A Balanced, Biblical Look at the Holy Spirit's Work in Our Lives* (Lake Mary, Fla.: Charisma, 2014), 156.

ABOUT THE AUTHORS

Rob King is the senior pastor of Vineyard Cincinnati Church in Cincinnati, Ohio. The Vineyard is an influential, vibrant community that has a rich legacy of service and compassion. Rob's mission is focused on sharing the Gospel message and encouraging people to passionately follow Jesus Christ. He graduated from Illinois State University with a background in social work prior to entering full-time ministry in 1997. He began serving as senior pastor at Vineyard Cincinnati Church in 2013. Rob and his wife, Stephanie, have three children: Jenna, Peyton and Caleb.

Eric Ferris has served at several influential churches, including five years with Rob at Vineyard Cincinnati. His 25-plus years of pastoral experience include executive-level leadership, twenty years of working with young people and more than ten years as a teaching pastor. Eric is known for his love for the local church, bringing clarity in complexity, and a straightforward approach to life and ministry. Eric and his wife, D'Ann, have four children—Michael, Courtney, Erin and Katie—and live in the Cincinnati, Ohio, area.

Both Rob and Eric play way too much Ping-Pong, laugh a lot and love being pastors. You can reach Rob at www.vineyardcincinnati .com and Eric at www.ridetheferriswheel.com.

Rob also has social media profiles that are handled by the church:

https://www.facebook.com/pastorrobking

https://twitter.com/robk1ng